Complementary Curriculum Approach

Transform Your Practice Through Intentional Teaching

Lisa Porter Kuh, Ph.D. and Iris Chin Ponte, Ph.D.

Exchange Press

ISBN 978-0-942702-77-4
eISBN 978-0-942702-78-1

Printed in the United States.

© Dimensions Educational Research Foundation, 2022

Book Design: Scott Bilstad and Chelsea Parker
Editor: Erin Glenn

This book may not be reproduced in whole or in part by any means without written permission of the publisher.

For more information about other Exchange Press publications and resources for directors and teachers, contact:

Exchange Press
7700 A Street
Lincoln, NE 68510
(800) 221-2864
ExchangePress.com

Dimensions Educational Research Foundation and Exchange Press cannot be held responsible for damage, mishap, or injury incurred during the use of or because of the activities in this book. Appropriate and reasonable caution and adult supervision of children involved in activities and corresponding to the age and capability of each child involved are recommended at all times. Do not leave children unattended at any time. When making choices about allowing children to touch or eat certain foods, plants, or flowers, make sure to investigate possible toxicity and consider any food allergies or sensitivities. Observe safety and caution at all times.

Acknowledgments

This book is the result of our exploration, research and experience in the field of early childhood education. When we met at the Eliot-Pearson Children's School, the laboratory school at Tufts University, we were both seeking ways to improve our classroom environment, teaching practices, and children's experiences without having to commit to just one approach. Our backgrounds brought various theories and practices together and we began documenting and sharing what we now call the Complementary Curriculum Approach.

Over the past 15 years, Complementary Curriculum has become part of our daily lives. It is robust, it is full of choice, order and flexibility, and most importantly, it offers permission to find joy in all things. We hope that as you consider Complementary Curriculum for your classroom, it brings you the same excitement and happiness it has brought to us.

Many people have supported the journey to bring Complementary Curriculum into the world. At every conference, workshop, consult, and talk we have been influenced by teachers, directors, and early education professionals. Their experiences and voices motivated us to improve our practice and incorporate all we learned. The following programs have had a significant impact on the development of Complementary Curriculum: Somerville Public Schools, Eliot-Pearson Children's School, Henry Frost Children's Program, Kendall Nursery School, Lincoln Nursery School, Charlestown Nursery School, Dandelion Montessori School, Open Center for Children, The Elizabeth Peabody House Preschool, UNH Child Study and Development Center, and the Somerville Partnership for Young Children. We extend our appreciation to the following individuals who gave us in-depth feedback and support along the way: Valerie Giltinan, Heidi Given, Claire Kamenski, Heather DiGiovanni, Debbie LeeKeenan, and George Scarlett.

Many thanks to Ann Pelo for her invaluable feedback shaping the narrative. We appreciate the faith and confidence of the entire Exchange Press team, providing support, encouragement and guidance as the book came into being.

Writing a book while working, raising a family, and running a school is no small feat. We must acknowledge and extend our appreciation and our love to our families for their ongoing support.

This book is dedicated to every preschool teacher who believes that early education should be better, and to every director who commits to improving practice in their program. Finally, this book is dedicated to children —who remind us to be curious, to wonder, and to love learning.

Table of Contents

Introduction
The Search for the Settled Classroom......................................7

Discovering a New Mindset

Teaching with Intention Means Teaching for Equity

The Power of Intention: Examining our Beliefs about Teaching and Learning

The Four Intentions: The Foundation of Complementary Curriculum Approach

Making the Four Intentions Visible

Early Childhood Legacies
The Influences that Shape Complementary Curriculum 17

Early Education Legacies: What Can They Reteach Us?

Bringing the Theories Together

The Prepared Environment
Old Norms, New Visions 27

What our Early Education Legacies Say about Learning Environments

Preparing the Settled Classroom: Beauty and Organization

Making Intentional Choices: Walls, Floors and Furnishings

Personalizing the Learning Environment: Rethinking Commercially Produced Elements

Conclusion: Environments Ready for Learning

The First Intention
Compelling Materials 51

Compelling Materials: Design Principles and Logistics

Four Key Ways to Offer Materials to Children

Conclusion: Integrating Compelling Materials

The Second Intention
Explicit Presentation 65
Setting the Stage
The Art of Explicit Presentation
Explicit Presentation for Individual Children
Explicit Presentation for Small Groups of Children
Explicit Presentation for Your Whole Group of Children
Categories of Presentations
Conclusion: Incorporating Presentations

The Third Intention
Responsive Scaffolding. 79
Scaffolding as a Foundation for Learning
Supporting Children through Scaffolding
Everyday Responsive Scaffolding Strategies in the Classroom
Conclusion: Looking for Windows of Opportunity

The Fourth Intention
Following Children's Interests 91
Learning from Emergent Curriculum and the Project Approach
Plan with Children's Interests in Mind
Consideration of Materials, the Prepared Environment, and Local Resources
Multiple Entry Points for Learning: Preparing the Environment
Conclusion: Following Children's Interests in an Intentional Way

Finding the Settled Classroom
Protecting Choice and Using Time Well 107
Why Choice Matters
Supporting Choice and Decision-Making: Why Time Matters
Conclusion: Time, Freedom and Joy
A Closing Message

References 121

INTRODUCTION

The Search for the Settled Classroom

"We are not sure what to do with this group of children! They just seem to tear apart the room. They are disruptive at circle time and disrespectful with materials. We are exhausted. We need help!"

What is happening here? Visiting a variety of classrooms, we see and hear teachers grappling with similar concerns: how to offer curriculum that supports children's ability to (1) engage in positive play, (2) negotiate social situations, (3) concentrate, and (4) manage emotions.

 Teachers are struggling to keep their classrooms productive—both calm and creative, energetic but not chaotic—it is a balance. Listen to the voices of some teachers we know.

> *"The children don't stay with an activity or really get invested in it unless I am with them the whole time, and I can't always do that."*

> *"I thought the things I put on the tables would be fun for them to play with, but all they do is argue over the toys and then move on to something else."*

> *"If I had more teachers or even a one-on-one aide for some children, then everything would run smoothly."*

> *"I want to do more inquiry-based learning, but I just don't have the time to fit it in. I'm too busy putting out fires all over the classroom."*

Teachers experience joy and success in their work every day, but many are also at a loss for how to solve some of these challenges. In trying to explain what's challenging in classrooms it is easy to fall back on children's behavior as the problem. "The children are being destructive with materials. They are basically dumping out the container and moving to the next activity without focus." In an effort to direct the energy in the classroom, teachers turn to rules and limits. When asked about the kinds of workshops or professional development teachers want, they often request support with behavior management—equating teaching with controlling children's behaviors.

All behavior is a form of communication. What are the children telling us? The children are giving clear feedback: "I am ready to play with something else but the teacher said I need to stay here and play with the LEGOS®." "I want to play with the Magna-Tiles® longer because I am right in the middle of building something interesting, but the teacher said I have to move to another table." "I am tired of sitting, I feel wiggly and need to move, but have to stay here at this center until the bell rings." Children's communication is clear: they want more engaging materials, with abundant time to play and explore.

Children want to make choices for themselves and have some agency over their own learning. They are communicating this developmentally appropriate need, which is characterized as misbehavior and sends teachers running around all over the unsettled classroom. Teachers try to get control of the classroom and the children's behavior by defaulting to worksheets, or having children move from center to center in 10-15 minute increments when the timer goes off, or plunking the same tubs of materials on tables or the floor day after day. Yet teachers aspire to a settled classroom where children are engaged in productive and joyful play. The intention is to keep the children focused and quiet and to minimize disruption, but it backfires as children push back on the constraints of the daily schedule, uninteresting materials, and limited choices. Most of the time, the problem of an unsettled classroom does not rest solely with the children. Often, the problem rests with teachers' response to the children and the classroom environment. But crucial to solving the problem is what comes *before* these moments of behavior management—how teachers prepare themselves, the environment, the materials, and what they will do and say when they are teaching.

The Complementary Curriculum Approach offers another way to respond to children's feedback, with intention rather than desperation. Our hope is that considering new ways of thinking about how to engage children in interesting, relevant learning experiences with compelling materials will help you on your journey to being a stronger and happier teacher, and that your children and families will benefit. This is not a prescribed, packaged curriculum. It is a lens you can apply to any curriculum you follow. The Complementary Curriculum Approach intentionally integrates a variety of approaches and philosophies and invites you to teach with multiple lenses as you plan for and with children.

Discovering a New Mindset

There is a felt dilemma between the traditional approaches to skill-oriented teaching and the desire to foster play-based learning. On one hand, early childhood educators want to promote play-based experiences and open-ended, creative opportunities with loose parts and multiple entry points, because teachers know that children learn through play and hands-on exploration (Copple and Bredekamp, 2009). On the other hand, teachers are under increasing pressure from administrators and funders to teach academic content and discrete skills linked to assessments that measure children's learning. Teachers feel caught in an either/or choice between play and skill-building, and they can become immobilized.

Children are often blamed for the chaos in the classroom. Administrators blame teachers for not being able to control children's behavior. The general population blames teacher preparation for not teaching educators how to manage their classrooms effectively. Teachers blame themselves for not being able to get the children settled and engaged. Society blames parents for not setting enough limits at home so that children come to school better regulated. At the same time, preschool curriculum can often look more like kindergarten or even first grade, as preschool joins the ranks of the K-12 world in

THE SEARCH FOR THE SETTLED CLASSROOM

COMPLEMENTARY CURRICULUM APPROACH

public schools. The mantra is about getting children "ready" for kindergarten, which in many settings means doing kindergarten in preschool. The reality is that kindergarten should look more like preschool if we really want to foster play-based learning! In the absence of concrete ways to shift thinking and practice, teachers, directors, principals, and even parents often become stuck in a kind of dualism: play or academics, freedom or structure, independence or collaboration. Yet there are ways for teachers to think differently about these polarizing features of educating young children.

The Complementary Curriculum Approach invites teachers to support children's play and cultivate classroom environments with rich, interesting learning experiences at the core. Under this approach, several key early education philosophies and theories come together in ways that complement each other, rather than divide our field into opposing camps. The Complementary Curriculum Approach offers intentional practices that teachers can use to structure the environment, design learning experiences, offer materials and establish routines in ways that create settled classrooms. A settled classroom is one where children are free to choose materials and experiences that interest and delight them, have the time and space to concentrate on meaningful, interesting activities, and work and play joyfully as part of a community of learners. The adults in a settled classroom are equally delighted as they thoughtfully guide children in their pursuits, following children's interests to deepen learning. The Complementary Curriculum Approach is not a series of defined lessons and predetermined activities. It is a way of approaching curriculum that builds upon the teacher's ability to personalize the environment and learning experience, with a steadfast belief that all children can learn. This approach involves observation of children's play, designing curriculum based on children's interests and passions, and planning responsively across content areas.

Teaching with Intention Means Teaching for Equity

The Complementary Curriculum Approach brings an equity lens to early childhood education. When teaching for equity, educators engage in the important work of helping children and families to ==develop a sense of identity in a diverse society== (Kuh, LeeKeenan, Given, and Beneke, 2016). This encourages children to be proud of themselves and their families, respect a range of human differences, recognize unfairness and bias, and speak up for the rights of others (Derman-Sparks and Edwards, 2010). If teachers are to truly meet the needs of every child, they must use a range of approaches—not one size fits all curriculum and routines. Relying only upon traditional and dominant approaches to curriculum, without an examination of how they impact all children, puts teachers at risk of overlooking the strengths and knowledge children bring to the classroom.

Without an understanding of how curriculum impacts children's social-emotional development and ultimately how children approach learning, teachers default to a limited set of practices, and their perspectives become narrow. Inevitably, there are children whose needs will not be met when the predominant choices are overly simplistic activities and teacher-centered activities. Also, if every offering is open-ended and requires collaborative social skills and children do not yet have the ability to share, they are set up for struggle. When the bulk of offerings involve teacher-directed, whole group instruction, children who crave and need independent choice and

individual opportunities are left out. If teachers offer children the same uninspiring materials day after day, with little scaffolding to spark curiosity and intellect, children in turn lose their own spark for learning. When children never have the opportunity to make their own choices, based on their own interests, they get the message that school and the learning process are imposed, adult-centered endeavors.

What teachers choose to study with children, and how they approach it, matter. There are children who will not see themselves in the curriculum because the focus is on themes and activities that are not relevant to their lives. In fact, some teaching practices actually infringe upon a child's right to an educational experience that reflects their interests and connects with their approach to learning. In contrast, the Complementary Curriculum Approach is inclusive in that teachers develop a deep repertoire of practices to reach every child. Every child has the right to a responsive early education experience which honors their cultural, social, and intellectual ways of being. This means teachers need to re-examine their values and beliefs about how children learn and about a teacher's role in meeting the needs of all children.

The Power of Intention: Examining our Beliefs about Teaching and Learning

The Complementary Curriculum Approach is built on several core values and beliefs. As you read these, think about how they align with your practice or provoke new thinking for you.

A teacher's job is to promote play-based experiences and open-ended creative opportunities, interwoven with academic, skill-based experiences.

Often in early childhood education, these are framed as completely separate endeavors, and teachers are encouraged to favor one over the other.

Children need to play and learn in ways that meet their inquisitive nature, curiosity, and developmental needs. Without play and inquiry that supports intellectual, social, emotional, and physical development, children do not thrive, and they do not learn to love learning. The Complementary Curriculum Approach values the importance of teacher-designed and child-led experiences that integrate a range of opportunities for children, allowing play and skills to peacefully coexist.

Meaningful curriculum follows children's interests and engages them in learning about what interests them, with materials that are inviting and compelling, at their own pace.

Teachers are under pressure to bridge the achievement gap, to meet accountability requirements, and to assess learning. These pressures often lead them to default to uninspired practices such as worksheets and timed centers. These are a problem because the learning sits firmly in the hands of the teacher, not the learner. Children have the right to make choices about what they want to learn, and how they want to learn it. Educators guide and support this, but not at the expense of controlling every moment of children's learning. The Complementary Curriculum Approach values learning that happens through compelling, challenging, relevant experiences, not only through teacher-directed, highly-scheduled, outcome-driven activities.

Children have a right to and deserve the time to tinker, build, experiment, and hypothesize so they can make discoveries and see themselves as investigators.

With the Complementary Curriculum Approach, children are given abundant time to explore materials and their properties and to create new ways of using them. Without these opportunities, learning becomes a series of fast-paced, weekly themes with little depth and short play periods in days full of transitions and filler activities. Really hunkering down with something interesting promotes perseverance

put these quotes w/ curriculum planning.

and an approach to learning that will stay with children long after they leave the classroom.

Explicit instruction and discovery can and must coexist, because intentional and strategic modeling and scaffolding actually support discovery and children's success with materials.
Contrary to popular belief, showing children how to use materials does not stunt creativity. Modeling presentations of how to use and care for materials supports inquiry, expands children's thinking and allows them to feel successful as learners. With the Complementary Curriculum Approach, teachers give a range of presentations, from how to care for and use materials, to more complex, multi-step, content-related activities to instill independence and confidence. These presentations support the free play and open-ended discovery that are vital to children's learning. The teacher's job is to scaffold all kinds of experiences in ways that foster successful engagement.

Play takes many forms; it happens all day, and everywhere, teachers need to tune themselves into children's play as a way to understand who the children are and what they care about.
Children have the right to play—imagining new worlds, taking on exciting roles, engaging in deep exploration of a material, engaging with nature, and testing their physical limits. Play is not just the housekeeping corner or block area, but happens in the sand pit, at lunch, and at the cubbies as kids put on their coats. Play is children's natural language; it's the way they explore and make meaning of the world around them. Wherever it happens, it is anchored in inquiry, discovery, and deep concentration. It is a necessary part of children's lives, and teachers' lives as well. The Complementary Curriculum Approach is built on understanding the value of play, and supporting it both in the classroom and outdoors.

How do these core Complementary Curriculum beliefs fit with your teaching practice? You may believe that children are capable, but you do not offer them a range of accessible choices in the classroom out of fear that they will misuse materials. You may believe that play is important but are unsure of how to create child-led play experiences or offer engaging choice time. You may believe that children are capable players, but you err on the side of tight control over activities and routines. The Complementary Curriculum Approach aims to align your beliefs with actual practices to bring joy and intention to your work and to children's lives.

The Four Intentions:
The Foundation of Complementary Curriculum Approach

The Complementary Curriculum Approach identifies Four Intentions that help teachers integrate these values and beliefs into direct practices with children. We define intention as a purposeful aim, plan, or provocation that guides teachers' productive action in the classroom. The Intentions are directly related to practices that all teachers can carry out daily as they work with children and develop purposeful curriculum. The Four Intentions complement each other and, when used together, allow rich curriculum to emerge. They are:

1. Compelling Materials

This intention focuses on how teachers can design and offer materials to inspire children's curiosity, experimentation, and thoughtful decision-making. It asks teachers to provision the classroom with interesting materials that are available for children to choose, and to add complexity to those materials over time.

2. Explicit Presentation

This intention introduces teachers to the practice of modeling the use of materials. It asks teachers to guide children to be purposeful with materials, and to build and sustain children's independence. This occurs through the practice of explicit modeling of behaviors, interactions, self-care routines, and the use of materials.

3. Responsive Scaffolding

This intention asks teachers to think about their supporting moves and interactions with children. It asks teachers to observe and listen to children so they can build upon and expand children's explorations.

This intention encourages responsive teacher language and non-verbal scaffolds to support children's success.

 4. Following Children's Interests

This intention asks teachers to plan provocations and experiences rooted in children's interests. Under this intention, teachers listen closely to children's wonderings about the world in order to develop curriculum with children that connects to their lives, communities, and fascinations. Teachers extend and enrich the exploration of Big Ideas with a focus on both child-led and teacher-inspired investigations that expand learning experiences over time.

Making the Four Intentions Visible

The Complementary Curriculum Approach braids the Four Intentions together into a strong approach to teaching. That braiding is visible with a green logo signifying the Four Intentions braided together and their increased strength when used to complement each other. The braid has no end and continues visually in both directions to remind you that this work is ongoing. Each person will have their own entry point to working with the Four Intentions and will focus on one or multiple intentions over time in new ways. The work does not end when you finish the book, but continues through your teaching journey. Green captures the organic nature of the Complementary Curriculum Approach, representing the natural course of children's development and the promise of growth and change for the educator. We hope that this image makes the Complementary Curriculum tangible and gives you a visual reminder of the Four Intentions—the commitments and practices that make up the Complementary Curriculum Approach. Teachers already engage in a range of practices that strengthen their ability to create meaningful, joyful play and learning experiences for children. We want to help teachers expand their repertoire as they set up beautiful, peaceful classroom environments. We want to help teachers feel comfortable giving Explicit Presentations about the use of materials while still providing open ended opportunities for how to play with them. The Complementary Curriculum Approach and its Four Intentions are vital to productive, developmentally appropriate practices in schools and classrooms. Teachers can offer freedom for play and inquiry without sacrificing structured, scaffolded experiences. Through careful consideration of children's learning and play experiences, these intentions support the development of children's ability to sustain focus and internalize their own possibilities for relationship and emotional competence.

The Four Intentions of the Complementary Curriculum Approach can be integrated into a variety of settings. Because the approach is inherently flexible and adaptable, it affords teachers the ability to create curriculum that suits their classroom setting, with practical strategies that can be adopted universally.

Our hope is that it helps you become the teacher you want to be, moving through the intentions to strengthen your unique voice and practice, to designing the environment and crafting experiences that inspire and energize your classroom. The Complementary Curriculum Approach paves the way for meaningful, joyful engagement for children, and for you.

Early Childhood Legacies

The Influences that Shape Complementary Curriculum

Early childhood education should be built on a strong foundation of theory that informs teacher practice. Unfortunately, in recent years teacher training programs have moved away from offering courses that introduce important contributors to the field. Also, in-service teacher training often focuses primarily on safety procedures, classroom activities, and compliance considerations. As a result, teachers are often at a loss to explain why and how they make decisions in their classrooms. Some rely on the way they were taught as children as the basis for their practice. Others rely on mandated rules from their school administration or licensing agencies to guide how they teach. Still others talk about intuition and instinct. Consequently, the field is adrift from the foundational philosophies that gave it shape. Remembering and reconnecting to core practices will help teachers consider how to utilize these foundational philosophies in their classrooms.

Early Education Legacies: What Can They Re-teach Us?

In classrooms in the early 1900s, there was block play, nature exploration, loose parts, high-quality wooden furniture, and real objects such as glass and china. These were regular elements of early childhood curricula, inspired by educational theories and philosophies. Although vestiges of these early environmental elements still appear in today's classrooms in the form of child-sized furniture and materials designed specifically for children, some are disappearing. There are classrooms today that do not have blocks and are filled with primary-colored plastic furniture and materials. These physical changes reflect the loss of understanding about the philosophies behind choices in material and environment. These choices shape the ways teachers interact with children. By reintroducing these philosophies, teachers can rediscover their foundational value to support children's learning.

The principal foundational philosophies discussed in this book include the theories of John Dewey, the Montessori method, the socially constructed learning experiences based on Lev Vygotsky's work and the practices of Loris Malaguzzi and the Reggio Emilia approach. We refer to these foundational philosophies as "legacies" because they have been handed down to us as valuable guides to enrich our teaching. These legacies, along with practical understanding and experience, are integrated into the Complementary Curriculum Approach. The legacies complement each other and can re-engage teachers in best practices that support children's growth and development. The legacies share a strong theoretical stance towards intentional teaching, to be reclaimed and called forward. While some aspects of these legacies have been woven into general early childhood practice, other aspects have been forgotten. The Complementary Curriculum Approach builds on what has persisted and brings what is less known to the surface.

John Dewey

John Dewey (1859-1952) was a philosopher and psychologist who was eager to understand how learning happens. Dewey was concerned about the dullness of rote learning, and he thought that the focus of education was not meaningful for learners. He hoped to create changes in how schools educated children and how teachers planned for and presented

curriculum. His ideas were a solution to subject-specific, rote learning, with children seated at desks in rows and a teacher lecturing at the front of the room, the version of school prevalent in the late 1800s.

Dewey believed that society as a whole benefits from an educational system that brings together the psychological, social, and intellectual aspects of learning and is inclusive of all learners. He opened a laboratory school in Chicago, where he and others grappled with big questions that teachers still discuss today:

- How do we prepare individuals to take charge of themselves, adapt to change, and shape and direct change in our world?

- How do we support children to think critically and act on their judgments?

- How do we support children's imagination and their experiences in the real world?

John Dewey's study and writing demonstrate that children need time to tinker, build, experiment, and hypothesize. "Hands-on learning," a term most early childhood educators use, is rooted in Dewey's observation that children learn through exploration. Important here is learning through experiences, particularly experiences relevant to children because of connections to their surroundings and context. Dewey's commitment to child-centered learning laid the groundwork for what are now known as emergent curriculum and the Project Approach. He believed strongly in following children's interests and offering experiences that meet each child's needs at a particular time in their development.

Emergent curriculum is a term rooted in Dewey's idea that the curriculum is not something that comes solely from adults (Jones and Nimmo, 1994). Rather, the teacher provides children with an intriguing, nurturing environment, interesting materials, and access to the outdoors, and then observes the children's play in order to base curriculum on the children's emergent interests. These topics often unfold over time, allowing for deep inquiry and investigation.

Emergent curriculum is also closely linked to project-based learning, also known as the Project

Approach, a curriculum strategy in which children actively explore real-world questions, challenges, and concepts through in-depth, hands-on investigations and research. These investigations might be initiated by children or teachers, and children can work in small groups, as part of the whole class, or even individually (Helm and Katz, 2016). The project approach has a complex but flexible framework that allows for different levels of experience and exploration (Katz, Chard, and Kogen, 2014). The integration of emergent learning and a focus on children's immediate environment allow teachers to create curriculum and set learning goals based on children's interests throughout the year. The Project Approach supports children's curiosity and can move in spontaneous and creative directions, central ideas of John Dewey.

Although Dewey was a proponent of child-led emergent learning, he also believed it was the responsibility of the educator to choose things that promote new learning opportunities for children and to select materials that inspire inquiry and deep thinking. How many students, Dewey wondered, have lost the impetus to learn because of the way they experienced learning? He argued that traditional education can actually dodge its crucial responsibility—to allow the learner to be engaged and joyful. He noted that "desks in rows, blackboards, and small uninteresting school yards" were not designed to connect with a community or to invite children into an environment for learning based on their own experiences.

Dewey's legacy is to keep things interesting and compelling for children and to draw upon their interests and life contexts for curriculum ideas. He pointed to the dynamic role of teachers: even as teachers keep the child at the center of the curriculum, they

Dewey's focus on hands-on, exploratory learning applies to a range of children's daily experiences.

have a responsibility to observe, plan, design, support and provoke learning experiences. For Dewey, education is a democratic right, where children are seen as competent and capable members of society. This mutually respectful relationship between the teacher and the child is at the core of providing equity in education.

Maria Montessori

Maria Montessori (1870-1952) was one of the first female physicians in Italy. She worked with children with disabilities. She developed materials and ways of presenting them that helped children who were deemed unable to learn to move forward with their education. Montessori focused on materials in many content areas, from Practical Life activities meant to support life skills (such as using utensils, tying shoelaces, and polishing silver) to materials to support sensory knowledge, math, literacy, geography and science.

Montessori viewed materials as valuable and foundational for children's learning. She became intrigued with how the methods she developed for disabled children would also work with typically developing children. As a result she was asked by city leaders to work with children in low-income areas of Rome. She opened the first Casa dei Bambini, or Children's House, in 1907. There, Montessori observed that when given the opportunity, children would most often choose materials and activities that were just what they needed for their phase of development. She also observed that children benefitted from instruction or modeling to learn certain techniques, social norms, and play skills. She developed explicit presentation routines for the materials she designed. She noticed that young children, rooted in what she called the "absorbent mind," would learn by observing others and then practicing with a material or experience over and over, until they mastered it.

Montessori's work teaches that children thrive when they have freedom within structure and can engage in work that is meaningful to them. This develops confidence and competence. She also believed that child-led experiences are completely dependent upon a teacher's commitment to see children as capable and competent, and to respect a child's right to her own pursuits and questions. This requires that children have time to choose materials, engage with them at length, and revisit them over time. Montessori classrooms emphasize opportunities for peer mentorship, and classrooms are organized across a range of ages or grade levels where children learn from and help each other in community.

Montessori felt that the classroom should be a "prepared environment" that inspires children's choice-making, and that it was part of a teacher's work to provision the environment for learning. In her prolific writing, the word *environment* is rarely mentioned without the word *choice*. She believed that children should be able to choose to work together or independently, and that the structure of the classroom and its furnishings and materials should allow for both (Montessori, 1967). However, *choice* in the Montessori philosophy means something very different from what is often found in contemporary early childhood classrooms.

In typical early childhood classrooms today, children work at "centers" set up by teachers with specific activities, or they choose from a limited selection of areas. For example, a classroom might have an art area, a dramatic play area, a block area, a light table, a writing center, or manipulatives set out on a rug. In contrast, in a Montessori classroom, children are not limited to activities put on tables by teachers. Instead, they can choose from dozens of activities, from simple to complex, arranged on shelves and curated in various areas of the room so that all the science, math or language materials are together. Almost all materials are available for children to work with during long periods of uninterrupted time, often up to two or even three hours. Time outside in nature is also considered extremely important.

Teachers arrange environments carefully so that children can function independently. Like John Dewey, Montessori felt that the environment should reflect children's lives and experiences. She included pictures of children, families, landscapes, flowers, and historical incidents, so that the environment would represent the children in it. Although developed in the last century, this perspective directly supports current diversity ideals as set forth in many environmental inventories such as NAEYC (National Association for the Education of Young Children) accreditation and ECERS-R (Early Childhood Environment Rating Scale) (Lillard, 2005).

Montessori emphasized child-sized furnishings and had tables, chairs, wash stands, and other items made for her classrooms. These furnishings, like everything in the prepared environment, were to be well-made and attractive. They were also meant to be moved by children to create flexible spaces for learning. She felt that children should be able to take tables and materials outside, connecting with nature as part of learning. She advocated for a simple aesthetic emphasizing beauty and neutral tones so children could feel calm, concentrate, and not be overshadowed by busy décor. Many of her "didactic materials," specifically designed to teach a particular concept or skill, continue to be widely available. Her legacy lives on in many of the ways we prepare classrooms today.

Many early Montessori materials are still used in classrooms today and are known for supporting engaged, focused learning.

Lev Vygotsky

Lev Vygotsky (1896-1934) was a Russian psychologist who explored the idea that all learning is socially constructed in some way—that is, learning happens in relation to others. His theories about learning and development have had an enormous influence on early childhood educators in a range of classrooms. Vygotsky championed the importance of play as the "leading activity" for the development of self-regulation and cognitive skills (Bedrova and Leong, 2006; Vygotsky, 1998). He saw the early years as a time when children's participation in play would lead to development in ways that would not occur when children were older. Through play children take on roles, try new language, and engage in new ways of thinking that help them learn to make sense of themselves, let others understand them, and collaborate with peers. In play, Vygotsky saw children often acting above their actual level of development. For example, when a child pretends to be a customer in a restaurant, the child experiences placing an order and interacting with the chef, developing important language and behaviors connected to these roles.

Vygotsky introduced the idea of the social context of learning, meaning that learning doesn't occur in a vacuum; children's learning is influenced by the place it which it happens, the people around the children, the cultures which make up the learning context, and the history of the community. All of this context impacts children's learning and influences a child's development. This is where some of Vygotsky's most important contributions surface. Vygotsky theorized that when children are exposed to the ideas and modeling of others, they move through what he called a Zone of Proximal Development, or the gap between what a child knows and what he or she can achieve with guidance and educational support. This means that when a child receives assistance or "scaffolding" through adult, peer, or environmental support, he moves from his initial level of

Vygotsky's idea that play and socialization are critical for learning applies to children across time and culture.

independent activity to a new level of independent activity. The concept of *scaffolding*—the coaching and guidance that help a child "move up a notch" in their skill level—comes directly from Vygotsky's theories, reminding us of the value of social interactions in a child's learning. Scaffolding a child's learning is not about "doing for" the child. Rather, it is offering concrete support that helps a child "build up," just like scaffolding allows construction workers to work upward. A teacher offers scaffolding by observing a child's level of skill and offering modifications to activities or the environment, or by specific coaching to support a child's movement to a new level of competence and understanding.

Vygotsky died young and his work was left unnoticed for many years, resurfacing in the late 1970s. This re-emergence of his work, combined with our knowledge about Dewey, Montessori, and the work happening in Reggio Emilia, commanded a new focus on the idea of developmental readiness for learning. Vygotsky is clear: teachers cannot simply wait for development to happen but instead must design, introduce, and provoke learning experiences. He urged teachers not to be bound by preconceived notions about what children can or cannot do because of their developmental stage, but to see development as a process that is always in motion, influenced by what is offered to children. Vygotsky's thinking opened the door for teachers to offer what in the Reggio Emilia tradition are known as "provocations," open-ended activities that don't have a prescribed outcome, to inspire curiosity and new learning. His ideas about scaffolding and guidance are critical to how teachers design and offer experiences that inspire learning and growth for children.

Loris Malaguzzi

Loris Malaguzzi (1920-1994) was one of the founders of the schools in Reggio Emilia, Italy in the late 1940s. His work was informed by a profound commitment to democracy and critical thinking, born out of the post-World War II rebuilding of the city of Reggio Emilia. Malaguzzi led his friends, neighbors, and fellow citizens of Reggio Emilia in rebuilding the schools in the city "brick by brick" from the rubble left after the war. They put children  and childhood at the center of this reconstruction effort, often taking groups of children to paint and play in public spaces to remind everyone that children were important members of the community.

Loris Malaguzzi recognized the power of children's ability to observe, experiment, and create.

Malaguzzi saw that, given the opportunity to engage deeply with materials, (or what in Reggio philosophy are often referred to as "languages" such as paint, wire, and clay), children could sustain focus on a topic for long periods of time. These extended pursuits using a range of materials foster children's capacity to raise questions, inquire deeply, and explore multiple perspectives in ways spoken language may not. Teachers work with children, usually in small groups, to develop projects of interest and meaning to children, using a range of materials to help children learn about themselves as learners. Malaguzzi believed that children's natural development and relationships with others should guide their learning opportunities. Through these projects and investigations, children and teachers act as researchers, co-constructing new understandings, discoveries, and connections.

Malaguzzi would have had a lot to say about current concepts of school readiness and children's place in society. He believed that children were already "citizens of the world" and should be visible, active members of a community from a young age. In this view, children are in essence "born ready" and the job of adults is to support their contributions to society. Teachers nurture children's interests and help them share their ideas—with each other, with adults, and with the community at large. Malaguzzi and other Reggio thinkers believed this is how a democracy should work because when children thrive, society thrives. These ideas about children as part of a democratic society stem from Dewey's work, and are an example of the legacy thinkers influencing one another.

In the schools in Reggio Emilia, children direct their learning by exploring, observing, hypothesizing, tinkering, and expressing themselves—ideas also drawn from Dewey. Educators scaffold, meaning they actively guide experiences to help children engage more deeply with materials and topics, tenets important in Montessori's and Vygotsy's work. In Reggio classrooms, teachers invite exploration of materials and, at the same time,

Reggio-inspired classrooms take up the idea that children respond to interesting materials complemented by novel provocations. The use of mirrors and light and shadow in these construction areas takes children's play to a more complex and sophisticated level.

offer careful guidance and instruction to help children understand their properties, know how to use them, and utilize them to ask questions about the ideas they're researching. For example, when children are introduced to clay, their initial experience is often simply to interact with it—poke at it, roll it, pound it, squeeze it—to get an idea of the qualities of clay. After they are familiar with clay, children might work in a small group with a teacher to explore how to build things like ladders or chairs or human or animal figures, thinking about what makes a sculpture stand up, or look realistic. Children are encouraged to ask questions of each other and give each other feedback as they work.

Children observing and talking about a snail are engaged in a key Reggio practice – group work. Malaguzzi recognized the power of children's collaborative sensibility when presented with interesting and relevant provocations.

In Reggio Emilia preschools, there is great emphasis on creating and fostering strong relationships among children, families, teachers, and the community. All of these relationships and experiences, Malaguzzi contended, were made stronger through "documentation." This refers to the process of telling the stories of children's and educators' thinking and research, through teachers' notes and observations, video and photographs of children's work and experiences, and teachers' reflections on the learning that is taking place. This is how educators develop new practices and explore new projects and questions. They share documentation to make learning visible to children, colleagues, families and the general public. This strengthens the community's identity as a group of people learning together.

The work of Malaguzzi and the preschools of Reggio Emilia inspire teachers to follow children's interests, offer compelling and interesting provocations, and think about the child's context: what in their local surroundings can be linked directly to the experiences children have in the classroom and the community at large? Malaguzzi asserted that children are already learners and already part of the society and community, and that teachers grow as educators when they learn from children.

Bringing the Theories Together

A common thread linking all these theorists is respect for the child's intellect and a commitment to every child's right to rich experiences. This is at the heart of the Complementary Curriculum Approach, which is grounded in these foundational legacies. Understanding and applying the components of these legacies provide a deeper understanding of how children learn and a richer repertoire of practices for teachers to draw upon. The Complementary Curriculum Approach is a bridge between the early education legacies, more recent research, and practical experience in the classroom.

The Prepared Environment

Old Norms, New Visions

How teachers set up their classrooms, from furnishings and materials to wall decorations and floor coverings, communicates what they believe about teaching and learning, and reflects their values about childhood. The classroom environment influences how children feel, how they interact with each other and materials, and how they behave. In many ways, the search for the settled classroom originates in the spaces that teachers design and offer to children. The settled classroom is a space where children are free to choose materials and experiences that interest and delight them, have the time and space to concentrate on meaningful, interesting activities, and work and play joyfully as part of a community of learners. Spending some time thinking about your physical environment will prepare you for the Four Intentions that are at the heart of the Complementary Curriculum Approach. Imagine entering a typical early childhood classroom, one that may be similar to yours or classrooms you have seen. Here are some things you may observe:

The door opens and your eye is drawn to brightly colored bulletin boards, each with a different-colored background and framed with scalloped borders of varying patterns. The flooring is red and white checkerboard linoleum tiles, with a rug covered in letters and numbers, and pictures that illustrate each letter of the alphabet—as well as a large sun in the center. There are other rugs in the room: one with a train track, one with a map, another with roads and cars pictured on it. The shelves are stocked with every type of material in brightly colored tubs. Some shelves have multiple trays, tubs, or boxes stacked on top of each other. The walls are decorated with posters of shapes, numbers, letters, weather and seasons, colors, and animals. One wall near the large rug has a calendar, weather chart, number chart, job chart, and a daily schedule, all in different colors and print styles.

On some walls, you see displays of children's craft projects, which look pretty much alike. Much of the furniture is brightly colored plastic.

The children are working at tables where tubs of toys have been placed: a bin of plastic dinosaurs at one, Magna-Tiles® at another, markers and paper at another. When the teacher rings a bell, she directs the children to rotate to another table to try a new activity for another ten minutes. This rotation repeats after ten minutes, ensuring that children have made it through all the activities. At the end of the last rotation, the teacher rings the bell again and tells the children "It's time to clean up and come to the rug!" Some children toss toys back into tubs, some children go right to the rug. One teacher begins singing with the children on the rug while another teacher moves from table to table, picking up toys from the floor and putting away tubs, then wiping down tables for snack.

There is a lot going on in this display! While colorful, the elements don't represent children's experiences and are largely adult made.

The classroom environment described above, while well-intended, raises some concerns because of the values and beliefs that are communicated and even fostered by the space. Compelling research shows that children's autonomy, choice, and sense of control in the classroom is linked to risk-taking, higher performance, and overall well-being (Lillard, 2005). The choices made in creating the space, intentional and unintentional, will impact how children learn, feel, and interact with each other in the classroom.

What our Early Education Legacies Say about Learning Environments

Early education legacies provide wisdom about the ways in which classrooms reflect the values of children, teachers, and the community. The legacies promote spaces where children can choose materials that meet their needs, and where their interests, identities, and feelings are visible and honored. This kind of classroom is stocked with interesting materials that promote exploration and inquiry. It is warm without being overwhelming, and the decorations mirror the children and the community where the classroom is located. It is important to reconsider some well-ingrained norms about what early childhood classrooms should look like and how they should be set up for learning. With guidance from legacy thinkers in early education, teachers can design classrooms that reflect their values about childhood and the teaching and learning experience.

Dewey and the Flexible Environment

John Dewey believed that teachers should see the environment as flexible, not "fixed," and should always be open to making changes to accommodate children's interests and needs. Dewey believed that classrooms can and should change in response to children's interests and that children should be able to access a range of materials to put their ideas into action. Think of the classroom he described as one of the first maker spaces! Photos of Dewey-inspired classrooms from the early 1900s depict elaborate pulley systems, giant ramps, and vast stores of art supplies around the classroom. Children are encouraged to collaborate to set up experiments, use materials in new ways, and engage in deep learning related to their interests. Now, when everything is bolted to the floor and wall according to safety guidelines, it can be a challenge to see the environment as flexible. But a flexible attitude is still possible, even while following fixed safety requirements. Over the course of a year, a teacher can change the classroom environment by changing what they put on shelves and how they arrange furniture to create new types of spaces.

Dewey's philosophy of experiential education and free play gave rise to the idea of "messing about" as a natural and necessary part of children's experience. If children were to truly learn through discovery, they would need ample time, space, and materials to explore. This freedom would allow children to experience the properties, cause and effect, and creative possibilities the materials offer. As children built huge structures with blocks, they learned about spatial relationships and the power of design. As they experienced nature and natural materials, they learned about sorting, growing and changing, and caring for the environment. Dewey described

Children need time to move materials around and experiment with them as part of learning in many different content areas such as building and art.

the classroom environment as an "instrument of agency," a space that allows children to "mess about" and capitalizes on their powers of observation and intelligence (Dewey, 1938). In this kind of environment, children could truly be active agents in their experience and reach their full potential as learners.

Montessori and the Prepared Environment

Maria Montessori coined the term "Prepared Environment" which refers to the process of intentionally designing learning spaces that are inviting and that offer a range of activities from which children can choose throughout the day. The prepared environment is more than simply supplying the classroom with compelling and meaningful materials—although that is important. It is a representation of our values about children's right to make choices about what they do and to be engaged in topics of study that are relevant and interesting to them.

Neutral flooring makes floor work inviting. The shelves are prepared with interesting materials for children to choose from.

Montessori described characteristics of the classroom that would promote choice, allow easy movement, and communicate a sense of calm and joy: clean materials, furniture arranged in an organized and orderly manner, with distinct areas of the room delineated for particular kinds of activity, stocked with materials that are neat and tidy. Montessori classrooms tend to have a more minimalist feel with not much on the walls so as not to distract children. At the same time, Montessori felt that classrooms should also feel "homey." This means different things to different people, but from a Montessori perspective a homey environment is welcoming and warm, and it is a place where you can concentrate. Montessori-inspired classrooms include living plants, beautiful objects like dried or

This child selected a tray from the shelf, took it to a workspace, and is actively engaged in the counting activity. When she is done she will return the materials to the tray and put the tray back on the shelf, preparing the materials for the next person.

THE PREPARED ENVIRONMENT

Floor mats create physical boundaries for children's choices, helping children to focus on their own work.

fresh flowers in ceramic vases, lamps to create soft lighting, and carefully chosen artwork and photographs. The classrooms also have clean furnishings and rugs in neutral colors like soft whites, beiges, or muted tones. In all of this, the priority is to create a space where children can move comfortably and without distraction as they decide what materials to work with. Montessori was also among the first to commission child-sized furnishings, originally made of natural wood, that children could move themselves. This flexibility to move around the space and move the furniture offers children comfort and ownership of the environment.

There is also a deep focus on the preparation and arrangement of materials. In Montessori classrooms shelving is designed to make materials accessible to

In a Montessori classroom, meals are designed with intention. Children help set the table, a practical life skill that supports independence, confidence and a sense of community.

children; everything that is on a shelf can be used by a child. Materials are spread out on shelves (not stacked) which allows children to easily take things off the shelves and put them away. It also contributes to a visually uncluttered space that is inviting and calming. The value here is that children can be trusted to choose the things that are most meaningful to them and that meet their learning needs.

Reggio Emilia and the Environment as the Third Teacher

In the Reggio Emilia philosophy, the classroom environment is called a "third teacher" and parents and educators are the other two teachers (Edwards, Gandini, and Forman, 1998). This captures the deep value that the Reggio approach places on the environment and the impact it has on children's experiences. In essence, the environment guides children to make choices, to engage with materials, ideas, and each other, and to behave in certain ways. Like Montessori classrooms, (Reggio founders were influenced by Montessori environments) the classrooms in schools inspired by Reggio Emilia are meant to be physically beautiful and arranged carefully and thoughtfully to draw children to activities. Reggio-inspired educators refer to these features as "provocations"— a material or experience offered in the environment to provoke inquiry and engagement. The classrooms often seem "curated," that is, selected and organized with a certain expertise and vision, reflecting the great care with which materials and children's work are displayed. Materials might be arranged by color or type of material. Documentation of children's work and the artifacts themselves are often mounted on black paper and accompanied by text and photographs that tell the story of children's endeavors. These displays capture children's thinking and the process of their work, as well as teachers' observations and reflections about the children's learning.

Branches collected by children become a provocation for a mobile, which becomes a provocation for the paintings on the table.

A simple provocation of beautiful stones to be placed on a tile, enhanced by natural light.

Each of the legacy thinkers advocated for children's participation in the arrangement of the classroom and the materials in it. Preparing a classroom is a process rooted in design principles and knowledge about how children learn and what they need. It is also an outcome of observation. A teacher observes what and how children are playing, what materials and activities they are choosing, and then designs and redesigns the classroom environment based on what is working well for the children and what might need tweaking. When you and your children collaborate to create a warm, welcoming, and engaging space, the environment becomes both a process and a product that impacts the learning experience (Kuh, 2014).

- Too much open space that encourages a lot of running? Time to create an inviting, well-defined area for more focused play by adding a small area rug and a small shelf for interesting building materials, or perhaps a low kneeling table for small constructions or art experiences, or a light table with a range of provocations, or pillows to create a soft space.

- Materials collecting dust on a shelf? Remove them and ask children to help you replace them with something more interesting.

There are many wonderful resources teachers can access for inspiration in designing the classroom environment. It is important, however, to be clear about the values you hold for your own environment before making design decisions. This isn't about designing magazine-worthy classrooms. Rather it should be about creating a learning space that reflects your goals and aspirations for yourself and for the children.

Preparing the Settled Classroom: Beauty and Organization

Designing classroom environments begins in response to this question: What do you need in your surroundings to do your best work? Take a moment to consider that now. Think about an ideal space that would help you think, be creative, explore a new idea, get some substantial work done, or finish a project. Consider what this space might look like, in specific detail; it might be at work, or at home, in your kitchen or at a coffee shop—someplace you would seek out because you know you would be productive and focused. What are the qualities and characteristics of this place, real or imagined?

A rug, natural light, interesting lighting, and a corner space offer a lovely spot for dramatic play.

Your list may include:

- a clean and uncluttered space, organized so that everything has a place and can be easily found and put back;

- quiet and cozy space to work with other people and alone;

- freedom to get up and move around;

- the ability to take a break from a project, without putting it away and then come back to it when you're ready to continue your work;

- natural light, or a view of the outdoors;

- beautiful things to look at;

- time to really dive into a project or activity. → schedule?

Don't children deserve the same conditions for their creative work and learning?

Are the things on your list present in your current classroom environment? Is your classroom environment a place where, if transported back to childhood, you could work, play, concentrate, move freely, and learn? If not, how might you create a classroom environment that is anchored by the elements on your list?

The settled classroom is a place where children engage in joyful and meaningful experiences. There are specific qualities of the prepared environment that inspire teachers to promote engagement and feelings of well-being. Often educators focus on the behavioral aspects of an unsettled environment—what children do when they push back against the constraints of scheduling, or the tedium of materials that don't spark interest. But teachers can influence children's behavior by how they prepare the environment and create a settled classroom. Beauty, also referred to as aesthetics, and organization are important foundations of classroom design.

Aesthetics

Aesthetics refers to the visual qualities of objects and environments, as well as the deep feelings associated with spaces and the objects in them (Flannery, 1977). There is a misconception about children and the idea of aesthetics, and in particular in early childhood education about what children's environments should look and feel like. One misconception is the idea that children need a "surround sound" of

Shelves stuffed with materials do not support the order children need to engage in calm, focused learning.

This overly colorful, over-stimulated environment can overwhelm children.

visually stimulating, primary color environment, in order to learn. The preponderance of primary colors in early childhood settings, while certainly its own aesthetic, doesn't take into consideration that children can appreciate and thrive in a more subtle palette of colors and textures.

Margie Carter and Deb Curtis note that cultivating a sense of aesthetics—the ability to experience, appreciate, and produce beauty—enriches children's perceptions of the world and draws their attention to things they might not otherwise notice (2008). There is no evidence that busy, cluttered, brightly colored classrooms positively impact learning; in fact, the opposite is true. Children who experience more minimalist-designed spaces, where materials are accessible in an intentional way, are more engaged and less distracted (Flannery, 1977). Children benefit from environments that move beyond commercialized images and the idea that only bright primary colors are appropriate for school.

The aesthetics of a space include not just the color of the walls or what is on them, but how the space makes you feel and what activity or mood it inspires. One exercise many teachers have found helpful is to do a primary color inventory in their classroom. After assessing the volume of primary colors in your room, consider areas where you could create a more neutral, softer environment. How might you reduce the overabundance of colorful patterns and designs on your bulletin boards, rugs, and furniture? Simple ways to change the overall color impact include using baskets instead of colored plastic tubs—or using plastic tubs in just one color. Instead of filling every space on a wall with posters and mismatched items, and overloading shelves with materials, keep the contents of the room minimal and allow for visual rest and appreciation of beauty.

Educators in the schools of Reggio Emilia consider aesthetics and beauty to be essential elements of the human experience. In their view, aesthetics are crucial in the development of empathy for other beings, places, and things because they can foster human relationships (Vecchi, 2006). The way a classroom looks and feels represents an attitude of care and attention. It also reflects how teachers and students make meaning of their explorations. The classroom should support curiosity and wonder. When children can play, connect with others, and engage with materials in an environment that is developed with care and attention to beauty, it communicates to them that they themselves are respected and cared for, and inspires them to care for materials and for one another.

Arrange the Environment with Order and Organization in Mind

A more minimalist approach to putting out materials helps children know exactly where to find what they

Note the child-created artwork at eye level on the art shelf and walls, as well as interesting elements hanging from the ceiling.

need and simplifies the process of putting things away. Montessori pointed out that children actually have a natural, strong sense of order. Try changing the order of a child's routine and you will see this in action! Reggio Emilia philosophy teaches the importance of offering children collections of interesting materials, organized in ways that offer the child the opportunity to enter into relationship with them. The chapter on Compelling Materials will focus on the design of the activities you offer. The chapter on Explicit Presentation will explore how to help children with routines for taking out and putting away materials. For now, focus on how you arrange materials on shelves.

offering them beautiful materials that are well cared for. It also communicates that adults and children take care of things in the classroom. Here are a few examples:

- When a material such as a peg board is taken out of the box and put on a tray, with the pegs in a small basket, the material is more inviting: children can easily see it and have a sense of what it is.

- Blocks should be organized according to shape and size so children can make construction decisions about what kind, and how many blocks to use. Having a cut-out of the block shape on each shelf helps children sort and organize the blocks.

- Tubs of manipulatives stacked side by side and on top of each other may be great for storage, but if children cannot see what is inside the containers, the material will lay idle, or be chaotically dumped out as children explore.

This jumble of materials makes it hard to see block shapes and means children need to dump everything out in order to find what they need.

When arranging materials on shelves, it works well to have one item per flat shelf space, to avoid stacking materials on top of each other. (Floor puzzles or games in boxes may be an exception.) If things are densely packed on shelves, children won't be able to see them or remember where they belong. Stacking and over packing materials on shelves causes boxes to break down, corners to bend, and things to fall apart. Presenting materials thoughtfully and with ample space honors and respects children by

One material per space makes it easy to make a choice.

THE PREPARED ENVIRONMENT

There is a long tradition in early education of labeling areas of the room, shelves, and containers of materials, often with pictures as well as a written label. This practice grew out of research on the importance of an environment rich in printed language. Exposure to written language is important, but labeling every shelf with a photo or word label is not necessary. If the shelves are neatly organized, with similar materials grouped together, children have no problem knowing where to get materials and where to put them back. If you use compartmentalized shelves that make it difficult to see what's inside the tub, you might attach a photo label to it, or put the tub on a more open shelf so a child can see into it. When the emphasis is on taking photos of all materials to use as labels, teachers are less likely to add new things. If the same things stay out for months, children who are ready for new challenges are not offered them. Yes, without labels, you may spend the first few weeks in your program year helping children know where to put things—time well spent on the road to a settled classroom. Offer small, respectful supports like whispering to a child, "When you are finished, that goes next to the pegs" or "Let me know if you need me to show you where that lives on the shelf."

Shelves for materials are set up for easy access. The blocks are arranged so children can see their shape and size. This makes it easy for children to clean up and prepare the shelf for the next builders.

Your classroom may already be set up in focus areas such as art, math materials, writing, sensory activities, science explorations, blocks, and dramatic play. As you organize each area, think of yourself as a curator. Curators are people most often associated with museums. They select, organize, and care for items in a collection. They think about what materials in a collection should be out for people to look at or use; they think about what would interest someone who interacts with the collection. While not a museum, your classroom is like a hands-on, rotating exhibit that requires thoughtful organization and presentation of the items in it. Your goal is to attract

COMPLEMENTARY CURRICULUM APPROACH

Children select materials from the shelves.

Traditional toys are organized for easy access, and to invite a range of play experiences. The materials are spread out so children can see the various objects and make a choice.

"visitors" to the shelves to interact with materials in meaningful ways and to make it obvious where things go and how to use them.

Children's natural sense of curiosity and desire to learn means they look for entry points into activities and experiences that are appealing to them. The goal in creating a settled classroom is to organize the environment so that children have choices rooted in their interests and the time to explore. This communicates to children that you trust them and are in tune with their needs. The key is to make materials as accessible to children as possible by organizing materials for child access. The organization of the space impacts everything, from how children and adults move within the classroom and use the areas of the room, to how children feel as they play. When children can move easily in a space and feel comfortable because they know where things are and how to access them, the classroom becomes a place of harmony. Now you are ready to consider even more details about the choices you make for furnishings, decorations, and materials.

Making Intentional Choices: Walls, Floors and Furnishings

Consider the colorful walls, floors, furnishings, and materials in the classroom described at the beginning of this chapter. For young children who are sorting out sensory stimuli in their world, the wash of primary colors and cartoon images can be overwhelming as they attempt to visually discriminate between materials, or try to concentrate on a project.

Walls

Cluttered walls covered with "surround sound" color and images create visual noise that some children (and adults) simply cannot block out. Walls are often used as archives—not necessarily a bad thing if items for display are carefully selected and serve a purpose, such as a mural of the neighborhood that has relevance throughout the year. But some walls are simply layered with "stuff" like snow pictures still up in the spring, anchor charts and multiple alphabet, number, color, and shape posters. Classrooms may have posters about appropriate behavior, and multiple worksheets or craft projects taped up on walls for months.

Certainly, rugs provide soft spaces for children to gather and can make for a warm and comfortable environment. But a room full of different colored rugs, some with designs like train tracks and roads on them, some with alphabet squares, is not so cozy; instead, it is overwhelming and loud. What messages do the busy designs send? Do children really learn their letters from these rugs? And what if a child wants to build something that has nothing to do with cars and trucks on the city rug?

Bulletin boards, each with a different color paper background and different scalloped borders, add to the visual confusion. Consider NOT covering each bulletin board with a different color butcher paper. Instead, use tan-colored butcher paper or something neutral like burlap. Consider leaving off the border altogether. Just let the children's work speak for itself. Intentionally decorating the walls with meaningful items, in an uncluttered way, provides "visual rest" for the eyes and the mind. For some children, the sensory overload of bright and busy walls leads to discomfort and a lack of engagement they cannot express in words, but communicate with wiggly bodies, unfocused play, and movement about the room without settling into a project.

Floors

Imagine a child working with multi-colored cubes on a multi-colored rug, trying to sort them by color. The wildly colorful rug, full of letters, numbers, and images, adds unnecessary challenge as the child tries to block out all that sensory stimulation. The effort of focusing on sorting and building with the cubes may soon feel like too much, and she may abandon the cubes, searching for visual and mental calm elsewhere.

One useful strategy for making the floor more inviting and practical for play is to use work mats or small rugs. Children can use mats while they work and play, to define space for materials. Note that this is not practical in the block area where large amounts of less defined space are important to promote expansive and creative construction. However, when children work on the floor with puzzles, baskets of loose parts or manipulatives, tray work, or clipboards, a mat helps define a space that children can manage and that other children can see and walk

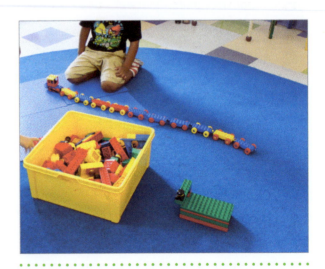

A simple rug invites visual ease as children play.

THE PREPARED ENVIRONMENT

Yoga mats?

You can store your mats rolled up in a tall basket, repurposed wastebasket, or umbrella stand. Carpet samples make good mats as well and can be stacked in a corner of the room.

Furniture

Often furnishings are a mismatch of items, due to budgetary constraints. However, try to streamline the visual impact of your furnishings as much as possible by sticking with one color or type. If you have multiple colored chairs and tables, can you trade the furniture with another classroom so that each has a uniform set of chairs and tables? Many companies make beautiful natural wood furniture that is lightweight, durable, and easy to clean. Natural wood also means there is less color to compete with your materials, which will certainly come in all shapes, shades, and sizes. A range of shelves with long, flat surfaces ensures room for materials of various sizes.

Ultimately, the classroom should be a flexible space that can accommodate children's social, emotional,

around. This saves materials from being stepped on and identifies ownership of an activity. Solid color mats provide a neutral surface.

Introduce children to caring for and using mats while they play.

- Invite children to a small group to demonstrate how to choose a mat, carry it, unroll it onto the floor and spread it out, roll it up, and return it to its place.

- At meeting, unroll several mats with space between them. Invite a few children to walk around and between the mats, demonstrating what this looks like. Ring a bell or chime and children can pretend to freeze during this walk, then continue walking until they hear the tone again, adding a listening component to this game.

A mat under a basket of materials defines a child's space while they play.

physical, and intellectual needs. Designing for each of these domains requires thinking about the ways we organize furniture and materials. Offering choice about how and where children sit sends them the message that the environment can be flexible to meet their needs. Space can be open and modified to reflect and support children's learning.

Often classrooms feel like a "sea of tables," and very large tables at that. Large tables are great for communal activities, collaborative projects and wonderful conversations at mealtime. But they don't offer children the range of options they need for their projects, like working on a project with partners, or having alone time for focused work. A few large tables that promote collaboration and large-scale projects can be combined with other tables to offer children a range of seating and work options.

One recommendation is to locate a shelf with activities near an open rug or table that can become a destination for the materials on that shelf. For example, you might locate the shelf of small manipulatives and fine motor materials next to a small 4-6 person table; children choose materials, and take them to the table to play. Children know when they go to that shelf, they use any of those materials on the table next to it. Some areas like the block, dramatic play, and art studios stay contained so that those activities maintain their own boundaries for focus and purposeful play.

Small tables can always be pushed together to create larger work spaces, something Montessori envisioned children doing to meet their needs. Lower the legs on small tables for a kneeling work space with small carpet squares around it. This opens up classroom space since there are no chairs at these low tables. Small low tables for two

Too many large tables combined means no space for individual and small group work, limiting the kinds of activities and interactions children will have.

Teachers split up their large tables into two distinct work spaces. They had red, blue, and yellow chairs but traded with another classroom so they had all red chairs to match their table and went with a gentle yellow wall color.

children invite more intimate partner play or allow two children to do quiet work side by side.

It is valuable to have a few small tables for one person scattered around the room. Some of these can even face a wall and hold a beautiful choice for children to work with, such as materials for observational drawing, a Lite-Brite® or peg board, or a set up for orange juice squeezing.

Low-level lighting in the reading corner invites quiet reflection on books and a warm home-like atmosphere that instills a sense of safety and calm.

These opportunities to work alone are often scarce in early childhood classrooms, but they are just as important as collaborative play, because they develop dispositions such as repetition, concentration, perseverance, reflection, and an internal sense of calm. Often, the only solitary place in a classroom is the "calm down corner," where a teacher sends a child who becomes disruptive. But children and adults need places for solitude and individual work, places of respite from the stimulation of the classroom and places of focus and quiet concentration.

Frames from a secondhand store await children's original artwork to create an ever-changing gallery of children's work. When children see their work displayed in a unique way and have a voice in determining what goes in their frame, they feel confident and proud of their abilities.

It is important that classrooms include a range of options for children's work.

Dewey and Montessori emphasize the importance of children being able to use the floor as a workspace, to lie down, to literally be grounded in their efforts. In one classroom, each child has a pillow in a unique color that they use for community seating around the large rug during group conversations; they use these pillows in other places during the day for cozy floor seating.

This room is designed so children have the choice to work in small groups, in pairs, or alone. The environment supports a range of activity and communication.

Large rugs become destinations to bring materials for solo work, pair work, and small group work. The small mats create little islands where children can gather and focus.

Figure 1 - Triangles

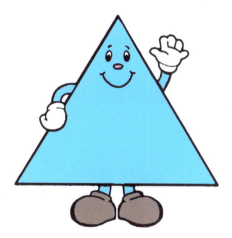

Personalizing the Learning Environment: Rethinking Commercially Produced Elements

With so many companies making items for early childhood classrooms, it can be hard to know what furniture and materials to choose. When you rely on an abundance of commercially produced, overly colorful and decorated items, you send a message that school is not part of our real world, but rather an artificial environment where only certain kinds of learning can take place. Some classrooms are full of decorations and multi-colored items from early childhood catalogues that don't represent the children, or the community, or don't create a personalized learning environment. Classrooms can move beyond anonymous and generic commercialized "stuff." Children can contribute to this move in meaningful ways, helping ensure that you design an environment that supports their ability to learn.

In the classroom that we described at the beginning of this chapter, the decorations on walls and shelves were added by adults without considering aesthetics, organization, or how children can contribute to the look and feel of the room.

Figure 1 is an example of the difference between a commercially produced classroom poster and one that was made by a teacher to reflect the children in the classroom. Look at the two triangle images. Consider the happy blue triangle with Mickey Mouse hands: how does it "teach" about shapes? The cartoonish face and body are a distraction and draw attention away from the shape, while sending a message that pictures need to be cute and silly for children to notice them, which is not true.

On the other hand, the children who made a triangle on the floor using their bodies probably gained a better sense of the properties of a triangle, because they participated in the experience and it represents them. Their understanding about triangles, gained from physically forming one, will be sparked each time they see the photo of themselves. The photo is a reminder of an activity they did together and the learning that grew from it. Children will be more interested in looking at themselves than at a store-bought cartoon. This is an example of a child-centered display, rooted in content generated by children, as opposed to a generic, commercial picture that is disconnected from children's classroom experiences.

COMPLEMENTARY CURRICULUM APPROACH

The teacher-made bulletin board (top) doesn't reflect the children or the community. The art display (bottom) includes photographs of children's work over time as they explored color using a range of materials and processes. It tells a story of children's learning.

Think about what is on your walls and where the decorations came from. You may have a calendar, an alphabet chart, a birthday chart, signs designating areas of the room, and children's names printed and posted on the walls. How do they reflect the real people in your classroom community? Are they commercially made? What changes would you make to create more child-centered, authentic wall displays? Instead of buying posters and labels, invite children to help make signs for the classroom. Instead of buying a calendar, write the names of the months yourself on poster board. Some teachers make birthday charts by taking photos of each child holding a sign with their birthday printed on it. What can you make, on your own or with the children, to create a classroom that reflects the people spending their days together in it? Moving from commercially produced materials to more authentic ones builds investment in the learning that happens as you create the environment together.

Aesthetic Reflection: Stepping Out to Set Up

Having considered how your classroom looks and feels in relation to color and pattern, order and organization, and child-centered elements, now take a deeper overall look. When the children are not in the room and it is tidied up for the day, step out of

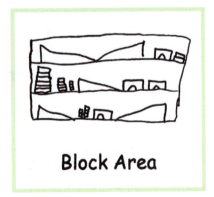

Teacher writing accompanies a child's drawing of the block shelf. Children can contribute to labeling the areas of the classroom, putting their own mark on the spaces. This cultivates an ownership and responsibility for the environment.

THE PREPARED ENVIRONMENT

your classroom, take a breath, and then re-enter, pausing at the doorway to really see your room. Consider these questions as you look and make some notes as you observe the space.

1. What is the first thing you see? What catches your eye right away, as you walk into the room?

2. How do you feel in your room? Energized, calm, overwhelmed? What elements of your room contribute to that feeling?

3. Consider the perspective of someone entering the room for the first time. What might they notice right away? What might they feel about being here for many hours a day?

4. What areas are you drawn to? What areas are most inviting? What areas feel cluttered?

5. How do the colors work together? Do they clash or complement each other?

6. Is there room to move? Too much open space?

7. Where would you want to spend time?

Now, review your answers. What aspects of your environment are working well? What might you modify? Where will you start?

Adding plants and flowers adds to the beauty of the space. Children appreciate living things in the environment and bringing nature into the classroom. The plants are another way for children to care for the classroom environment and feel pride in the space.

COMPLEMENTARY CURRICULUM APPROACH

The teachers in this toddler classroom engaged in a primary color inventory, adding neutral wood furnishings, logs instead of plastic shapes for indoor gross motor play, and neutral rugs to create areas to gather. Note children's artwork and documentation of children's learning around the room.

↑ stumps/logs?

Focus on redesigning one small area. Some teachers start with the primary color challenge, attempting to move away from primary colors as the main color scheme of the classroom. You could start with the images on the walls. Remove everything from the wall, even the borders and colored paper from display areas. After getting a feel for the open space, begin to add things back to the walls, emphasizing children's work, photographs and text that tell the stories of children's learning, and artifacts that capture the life of the community in and out of the classroom. Mount children's artwork on black paper to frame it, and include photographs next to the artwork to show the children at work.

Some teachers start with their shelves, clearing off one shelf at a time, inventorying the items so they really know what they have to work with, and replacing one activity in each available space, without stacking materials. You could add some plants and small lamps to the shelves to create beauty and softness. A similar strategy is to start with the storage areas for materials that aren't being used, organizing them so you have room to store things that you remove from the shelves children access. However you decide to start, make it something achievable that brings you joy and ease.

Conclusion: Environments Ready for Learning

Throughout this chapter we prompted you to think about how you feel about the spaces you work in and the environment you offer to children. What do you need from your surroundings to do your best work and learning? What do the children need? This is about more than beautiful classrooms painted in soft tones. It is also about children's access to prepared environments that are interesting, spark independence and agency, and are happy and joyful places to learn. This kind of environment should be a right for every child. With intentional guidance children can be trusted to make decisions about what they want to play, where they want to play, how they want to play, and who they want to play with.

Understanding the concept of the Prepared Environment and all that goes into it shifts teachers' thinking and develops their own sense of agency. Teachers deserve the ability to curate their own classroom environments. Trust yourself to develop the awareness and intention needed to make careful choices about what goes on the walls and what furnishings and materials are provided for the students and the community you serve.

THE FIRST INTENTION

Compelling Materials

Designing for Choice and Discovery

In the morning, the teachers enter the classroom and turn on the lights. They consider the bins of materials on the shelves. They pull out one bin of DUPLOS® for one table, sheets of white paper and crayons for another, and a few Mr. Potato Head™ toys with pieces for the third table. Now the classroom is ready. Children arrive and move through the room, trying out a few activities, but after the initial rush to play, they quickly lose interest and get silly, running around and between the tables. The teachers are frustrated, and it shows as they try to regain control of the classroom. This is exhausting—and it happens almost every day.

In early education, "centers" are a mainstay of how teachers offer materials and activities to children. Teachers place materials on tables, or perhaps on a carpeted area or even on the bare floor, and send children to those spaces to play. In too many classrooms, teachers tell children where to play, how long to play there, and when to move to another play area. In theory, centers are supposed to allow children to make choices. In reality, centers can limit the selection of activities that teachers make available—which are often not very interesting to the children. This is where the Compelling Materials intention comes in.

Compelling Materials evoke interest and sustain attention, inspire curiosity and experimentation, and invite children into increasingly more complex interactions with materials and each other.

This chapter explores how to (1) intentionally choose materials, (2) set up classroom shelves and interest areas with materials that allow children to make their own play choices, and (3) use classroom materials as provocations that spark new interest and inquiry.

Offering Compelling Materials can have a profound impact on teaching and on children's experience in the classroom.

Teachers have described feeling like harried and tired servers in a very busy restaurant. They move from table to table to direct children's use of materials, and they don't really have time to engage in the interactions that foster learning.

Here are two examples of common challenges. Think about how these real stories play out in your classroom and what they reveal about how children engage with materials and concepts.

DUPLOS® Dumping

Jacob made a beeline for a huge milk crate of DUPLOS® that was on the rug in a corner of the classroom. Chronologically 4 years of age, Jacob was developmentally much younger, about 18 months. He did what any typical toddler would do, he dumped the DUPLOS® on the floor, sending hundreds of pieces scattering across the rug. Now, Jacob really wanted to toss the DUPLOS® into the crate in a classic version of toddler dumping and gathering, but the sheer number of pieces quickly overwhelmed him. He flung himself to the ground, rolling his body on the DUPLOS®, not knowing quite what else to do.

Experienced teachers always nod knowingly at this story about "dumping." It is a common behavior and an important one, as children to learn about cause and effect and to explore materials and their properties. However, dumping can quickly become a challenge when there are lots of pieces to manage. It can be overwhelming for a child faced with too many small pieces to navigate. When teachers pare down the sheer volume of materials they offer, children will be better able to successfully put their ideas in motion. For many children, less is more. To help Jacob get back on track with his game, his teacher quickly scooped up and removed about three-quarters of the DUPLOS®, made stacks with some of the remaining pieces, and watched as Jacob worked enthusiastically to pull apart the stacks and toss them into the crate. When the clean-up bell rang, Jacob put away the remaining DUPLOS® cheerfully, albeit with some help.

The next example demonstrates what can happen when children are repeatedly exposed to materials with little direction or provocation.

"Fun" with Bristle Blocks®

Circle time was over and the teacher directed the four children in the Blue Group to the table with the tub of Bristle Blocks®. It was the fourth week of school and the routine was the same: go to the table, play for a short time, move to another table when the teacher rang the bell, and play with something else. Repeat. At first, Bristle Blocks® were kind of fun, as were the playdough table and the puzzle table. But by day ten, the Bristle Blocks® had lost their luster. Throwing them or hiding them under the table suddenly became more interesting for the children. The teacher was exasperated when she saw how they were using the blocks.

Children choose what they want to play with and take it to a table.

This example also gets knowing looks from teachers. It is easy to frame this as a story about children's "misuse" of the blocks, which results in children in timeout or materials being removed. However, it is also a story about teachers and materials. First, the children didn't actually have a choice about what to do—the teacher put out the Bristle Blocks® and directed the children to play with them. When children don't have a choice about the materials they use, they try to find their own ways to interact with materials, eager for some sense of choice in the matter. Secondly, offering the same materials in the same way, day after day, can create boredom, which stifles creativity and discovery and can inspire destructive behavior as children try to spark some new energy from the dull materials.

Filling your room with Compelling Materials does not require you to go out and buy lots of expensive items; you most likely have many things you need right in your center or school. Reggio Emilia-inspired classrooms and Montessori-inspired classrooms use trays and baskets to organize materials. Take the time to choose from the materials you already have. Then prepare/design them in an interesting way that will entice and evoke children's interest in your classroom.

Compelling Materials: Design Principles and Logistics

As you develop materials, think: How long would a child work with this? What would attract them to it? Why would they play with this? This mindset is important because, when considering how to offer the materials to children, you need to have an awareness of how your children will take it up. It is also helpful to know what the children enjoy and what they are interested in. When you are inspired and motivated by the children in your class, designing different activities is motivating and fun.

Start with Storage and Your "Stuff"

Start with your closet and storage areas. You probably have more than you think you do. The first step of any good "clean up" is to get all your toys, games, and materials out, into a large open space. While overwhelming, this is a very important step because you can see how much you already have to work with. The next step is to toss what is broken, shabby, or missing pieces. Materials speak to children, so if an object is disorganized or missing things, it tells children, "I am not cared for anyway, be rough with me!" Putting broken or uncared for materials out in your classroom is almost an invitation for the child to continue to disrespect and mishandle the materials.

Now look at the materials that remain and determine which are still attractive to children. Are they worthy of children's interest? When you look at your materials, both your "keep pile" and your "toss pile," ask yourself: can they be repurposed in a different way? Can pieces of a game board be used as an interesting provocation with playdough? Can the gingerbread figures from an old Candy Land® game become an instant hit on their own? Can an old calendar be cut up for collage pieces? A note of caution here—be careful not to slide into a "keep everything" mentality and use care when deciding if things should be salvaged.

A large range of materials, from pre-packaged traditional preschool items, to beautiful found objects, to Montessori materials, provides a wonderful variety. Also be sure to keep a collection of containers—dishes, small boxes, baskets—to hold small items when you use materials with multiple parts or tools. The most important thing is that what you use is clean and well maintained. Secondhand stores provide a selection of baskets and trays, or you can ask for donations as families do spring cleaning. The ordinary items you may already have can be used in unique and interesting ways as you develop and design materials.

COMPLEMENTARY CURRICULUM APPROACH

Teacher storage area

BIG PROJECT!

Organize and label everything in your storage area—from pencils to small tongs, from trays to puzzles, from manipulatives to plastic animals. It is also useful to have large plastic see-through bins with labels and lids so you can see what you have when your bins are stacked on a shelf. Remember that your teacher storage is not the same as shelving for materials for children. Teacher materials are ideally out of sight in a separate cabinet, covered shelf, or closet. When you have a range of materials at hand, and they are organized for easy access, it makes it easier to quickly design and put out new activities. Go for it!

Designing and Testing

Now you are ready to design materials that can go directly onto your shelves or at a center for children to choose. Teachers find the design process gratifying as it lays the groundwork for children's learning and for teachers to extend initial designs over time. The following steps give you a pathway to the design process. Ultimately you want to design for simplicity and yet offer a new challenge, working with one area or material at a time.

Review the material and the learning goals:

It is important to come to the design process with ideas and goals for what you want to offer as a provocation for children's learning (Curtis and Carter, 2008). Your design could be centered around a material—for example, pattern blocks, a common classroom material used for exploring shapes, spatial relationships, and patterns. What do you want children to do with the pattern blocks, and how can you offer them to children, beyond a huge tub? A partitioned tray, with a different pattern block in each section, supports ease of seeing each shape and open-ended building; a basket of shapes with outlined cards supports matching and scaffolded designs. Offering only hexagons, trapezoids, rhombuses, and triangles with outlines of hexagons supports seeing how different parts can make a whole. Thinking about the concept you want children to explore and the materials that support that concept brings even more intention to what you will design and offer.

Curated LEGOS® support visual novelty and discrimination, while sorting them on a partitioned tray helps to see each shape and encourages free building. The solid color rug makes color identification easy.

You can also design around a concept such as sorting or mark making, or an interest of the children such as color or plants. If your goal is to build on children's interests about plants and engage them in new discoveries, imagine a shelf with green trays, each containing an activity related to plant life—for example seed sorting, observational drawing of plants, leaf rubbing, and shape punching with leaf shapes. A small plant and books about plants on bookstands might also be in this area. Design choices like these create a mood or tone, draw children to the activities, and help them experience the connection between the materials, where they live in the classroom, and what kinds of engagement they inspire.

Consider design logistics:
Who will use this activity? What kind of container works best? Where should it be kept? Where do you hope it will be used? These logistical considerations go hand in hand. Decide whether you are designing for a single child or small group. If one child at a time will be using the material, consider the number of objects on the tray and how the child will clean it up for the next child. If you're envisioning a small group, consider how many pieces each child will need to successfully experience the work.

Think about what kinds of containers are best to support ease of use, where the container will live in the classroom, and where a child will play with what you designed. Does the material go on a tray, or in a basket? Does it work best for children to use the materials on the floor or at a table? Will they need a mat at either the floor or table to keep the materials in place and organized? Are materials given enough space on a shelf so children can get them easily and put them back without piling things up or spilling them? Think about ease of movement from toddlers to older children and what they will need to successfully manage moving materials in the classroom. Try out how materials fit on a tray and how various-sized boxes, dishes, and trays can be combined to contain materials. Attention to these details will make it easy for children to facilitate clean up and reset materials for the next friend.

Tools such as vocabulary cards, magnifying glasses, half sheets of paper, and a simple selection of colored pencils add interest to an observational drawing activity.

It is important that each material has its own space and can be seen easily by the children, as opposed to things being stacked up or askew on shelves. Is it "table for one" work at a small low table where one child can concentrate? Is it a center where you might remove materials at the end of choice time and put them out again the next day? Does this material live on a small stationary table where children visit it? Think about where children might take materials once they have made a choice. Often the furnishings in an area become the designated spaces for certain materials. The large table in your art area becomes a studio space, and that is where watercolor painting will happen. The table in your writing area becomes the writing center table where children gather to write and illustrate stories. Other areas can be more fluid such as a shelf with math materials that can be taken to a nearby table or to work mats on the floor nearby.

Test your design.

Once you have created the activity, be sure to try it out. Ask yourself, "Do I have enough materials, the right kind of materials? Does the activity work? Will children be successful?" Sometimes what looks great to a teacher may be difficult for the child. Create a provocation and ask a colleague to try it, to see how it works for someone with a different lens and intention. When you test out the material ask, "Does it provide the intended challenge? Is it too easy, too challenging, or just right?"

Keep materials tidy.

Each morning, or even the night before, do a loop around your classroom to straighten the materials so the room is reset for a new day. Bring baskets, trays, boxes, or tubs to the front edges of your shelves. Straighten things so they look organized and approachable. Make sure things aren't stacked up and concealed. Is something literally gathering

↳ sensory bins

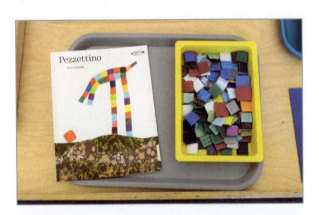

Trays, dishes, and baskets organized and available make it easy to switch out activities according what children are interested in and ready to learn.

COMPELLING MATERIALS

dust? You will need a range of well-cared for and clean materials, as well as ways to offer them, to meet the needs of your diverse learners. When materials are clean and tidy, the children will treat them with more respect.

Rotate materials and add complexity.
While design plays a crucial role in helping children experience new challenges, the rotation of materials is equally important. As the weeks go by, you will change and add to the repertoire of materials, depending on what the children are playing with and thinking about. Maybe something is not being used much and has run its course. Replace it with something else, or just change the tray, or add something new to spark interest. The rotation of materials is in essence your scope and sequence—a thoughtful progression of activities that meets goals and objectives for children's learning and responds to their emergent learning. What will you tweak or add to this activity to make it even more compelling, once children have achieved mastery? Where does this activity fit in the learning trajectory? Think about materials that will stay out all year either because children will eventually do more complex things with them, or because you will present extensions that provide new challenges.

As an example, consider this math shelf (Figure 2). Notice the variety of materials and activities for children in a small space, each with its own lesson and provocation for the learner. Objects are organized in a way that allows children to see possibilities. On this shelf there are plenty of interesting opportunities to take up. The educator can continue to add, extend, and change the options here as the year progresses.

Four Key Ways to Offer Materials to Children

Now that you have spent some time designing and preparing the materials and activities children will use, we will explore a variety of ways to offer materials. You may already be using some of these strategies, but as you read, think about how you will complement your primary modes of offering materials with other ways that might be less familiar. Your unique group of children will help you determine how many opportunities you offer, what kind, and when to offer them. Consider these four ways to offer materials and be purposeful about how and when to give children access to these opportunities. Children will need all these offerings to meet their needs. As you get to know your learners it will become more and more apparent what kinds of opportunities they are interested in.

Figure 2 - Math Shelf

57

The four key ways of offering materials are:

1. Materials at a center with minimal provocation.

2. A center with a compelling provocation.

3. A "gather here" shelf that inspires choices of loose parts, supplies, and materials.

4. "Tray work" arrangements of activities on trays, intentionally designed around specific content, topics or themes.

These four ways or "modes" move from simple to complex, but they are not meant to be exclusive of each other. In fact they must coexist, as children need multiple ways to access materials. All classrooms should have opportunities for all four modes of accessing materials.

Center with Minimal Provocation

In this mode there are minimal provocations, and children are mostly exploring materials from bins or baskets and making discoveries about their properties. Many teachers choose this approach for times of day that require a faster transition, morning arrival or close to departure time, when there might be a smaller group, as children are entering or exiting the program. This mode is the easiest to set up and break down and cultivates a sense of community at the beginning and end of each day. A center with minimal provocation (aka bin work) can make early morning set up and end of the day clean up a snap. Aside from easy set up and clean up, there is great benefit to this style of exploration for children.

When children "paw through" materials they have the opportunity to search and sort pieces. This experience can lead to categorizing, building, and constructing. As children use materials together they learn to share, collaborate, and negotiate. These are important skills that all children need to develop. Even when children are offered bins of materials, teachers should be thoughtful about the quantity. There shouldn't be too much or too little, so that multiple children can have access and engage.

Center with a Compelling Provocation

Another mode is to create a center with a compelling provocation. This means that the teacher has prepared an activity with more intentionality. For example, the teacher used the pattern blocks from a tub on the shelf to invite children to explore

Tubs, baskets and containers of loose parts support children's discovery, and sorting.

how beehives are designed. The teacher offered a non-fiction book with photos of a real beehive and grouped pattern blocks to suggest how beehives look. The teacher established the space to work with a black piece of felt to call attention to the invitation and highlight the honeycomb shape. In addition, the teacher added small plastic bees so the children could play out what happens in a beehive.

Once a week or so rotate in new materials. Offer multiple sets of an activity, for example this one featuring photographs of places familiar to children and objects to place and count, combining an opportunity for math and expressive language.

Using pattern blocks to explore beehives.

In this mode the teacher curates or arranges materials to promote new ways for children to interact with a selected set of materials. These types of opportunities can be connected to a topic or exploration the entire class is experiencing, inviting children to explore and discover more about a topic, in this case bees and how they live. By pairing the materials with a non-fiction book, children can play out something they have learned from a text. In addition, if the teacher wants to extend this experience, the teacher can add small bee figures to create a small dramatic play experience. This offers children another level of engagement with materials they already have access to in the classroom.

Compelling Provocation in Other Classroom Areas

In addition to considering compelling provocations as a tool for table choices, you can apply the same mindset when preparing other important areas of your classroom. Remember, less is more. Children can be overwhelmed or overstimulated with too much "stuff." Carefully chosen, clean, well-organized, and engaging materials go a long way. Consider how Compelling Materials can be applied in these areas.

Dramatic Play

Dramatic play is important to classrooms but often results in disorder and behavior management challenges. The teacher should carefully select items for dramatic play. Dress up clothing should be stored so that children can see their choices, put them on independently, and hang them back up when they are finished. Play food choices should be placed in a bin where it's easy to see what is inside, and not be piled high. Baby dolls should be carefully dressed with clothing that is easy for young children to take on and off. Just like the materials on the shelves, dramatic play materials should be rotated, arranged, and considered. The objects can match an area of exploration that the class is interested in. If playing with babies and play kitchens seem to have run their course, change things up. In many

COMPLEMENTARY CURRICULUM APPROACH

classrooms dramatic play can become so much more—a pet shop, airport, post office, or puppet theatre. Materials should come and go based on the children's area of inquiry.

Block Area

Just as with dramatic play, block areas can be very difficult to manage but are a crucial part of children's play experience. Turning a block area into a space of compelling provocation inspires children's ability to build and learn about the properties of blocks, while supporting successful navigation and clean up. First, be sure that the shelves holding blocks are clearly labeled and there is space for blocks of every shape and size. Initially, you may want to limit the number of blocks on the shelf as children learn how to take the blocks off, build, and put them away. Perhaps only two to three children build at one time so you don't have large numbers of children vying for a few materials. Gradually you can add more blocks and more children can play. Block areas can be more interesting when the props paired with blocks are connected to the children's interests and to what you are studying as a group. Rotating cars, animals, people, and beautiful gems can reinvigorate the area. Again, compelling provocation asks you to consider how much and what to have available to children.

Simple blocks in varying lengths and colors inspire interest and new ways to build when offered in color family baskets adjacent to a low workspace.

The organized block shelf makes it easy to creatively build and clean up. Adding props like street signs and road tracks inspires even more complex play.

Reading Areas and Library Areas

When choosing materials for the reading nook make sure there are an adequate number of books that are well cared for and not missing pages. Reading areas should also have a cozy place to sit alone or with peers. Books should be stored in a way that children can access them and put them away. Rotate and curate what books are accessible, making connections to the children's interests, classroom investigations, and level. Many teachers also like to make a book available to children after it has been read at circle time so children can reread a familiar story, perhaps making multiple copies available. Just like the materials available to children on the shelves, this area should be attractive and welcoming. Books should be refreshed and in good condition.

Gather Here

The "gather here" mode invites children to gather materials and create. This art shelf (Figure 3) is in a public school kindergarten class. Materials are organized so children can both see and access a range of open-ended materials, including different

Figure 3 - Art Shelf

kinds of paper, writing tools, stickers, and tape. Maker spaces, writing centers, and art and science areas often have this "gather here" mode of offering materials, and children can use their own imagination to decide what they want to create. Some teachers set up these areas almost like a grocery store. Children can get a basket or tray and approach the shelf to choose materials. Once they have an idea in mind they can choose the materials they need independently, carefully deciding what to put in their basket. Using the resources offered they can sort, discover, invent, combine and create. In order for children to learn how to use these materials properly they will need Explicit Presentations, which will be reviewed in the following chapter. "Gather here" spaces are a good way to encourage group work and collaboration—a child may choose to create something on their own, with a friend, or with a group.

Children can go to the art shelf and access materials to draw, paint, collage, or create 3D sculptures. Children can work at the writing center counter or gather materials to take somewhere else.

Tray Work

Tray work is the most intentionally designed mode, and the opportunity that may seem newest to you. A tub or basket of loose parts can be put on a shelf for a child to choose, but for tray work, each choice is arranged for a specific purpose (i.e. watercoloring, counting, cutting, or writing letters). We refer to this as "going from tub to tray" because sometimes the same materials offered in a tub on a table are made more complex and inviting when offered on a tray. Tray work creates opportunities for a higher level of engagement, often with more specific goals in mind related to what you are studying, and specific skills and content. In this mode, more structure shapes and guides the interaction a child has with the material. Tray work aligns children's choices with your goals for their learning over time, while maintaining a connection to classroom interests or a child's emergent needs. Arranging materials in smaller doses on trays, and designing for different possible uses, helps children stay organized and guides them so they can be independent and self-directed.

Color-themed offerings let children focus on the unique variables of each object and how they fit together.

Initially, arranging materials in this way may seem more limiting, and teachers often wonder if children's creativity will be stifled. This shouldn't be a concern because this mode actually fosters children's ability to successfully make choices for themselves and builds confidence and competence as children experience success. When work is presented on a tray with a reduced number of materials, children can find the activity more manageable and approachable. When children take up the opportunity and find success, they become more confident to take on more challenges. In addition, with a reduced number of materials they are able to reset the choice independently and prepare it for the next friend. When children are able to care

Painting can be set up for one child using a small tray, and a limited number of colors, and brushes.

for their own classroom materials, they have more ownership of their classroom space, choices, and learning—a powerful experience. Teachers spend less time cleaning up the classroom and have more time to focus on supporting children's learning.

For example, consider a large bin of building straws. The sheer amount can be overwhelming and lead to a more disorganized experience. In the image to the right, the teacher has offered less of the same material, storing the connector pieces separately to offer more organization and structure. This offers the guidance and support that many children need.

The container offers a way to organize materials, but the tray supports choice and structure, which can lead to increased concentration and creativity.

Fewer straws on a tray with links accessible.

Open-ended art opportunities can also be offered on a tray rather than spread across a table with no organization. For example, collage—for this activity you can create a tray with a variety of materials and tools. Children will be attracted to the order of the tray and be able to see all of the possibilities in an organized way, which will result in more creative opportunities.

Conclusion: Integrating Compelling Materials

The thoughtful planning and design of Compelling Materials is an important aspect of your Prepared Environment. The Prepared Environment enhances the structure of your classroom space, and Compelling Materials spark children's relationship with the things you curate and offer. Carefully designed materials promote engagement and independence, allowing teachers to move away from the harried server we met at the beginning of the chapter.

The question and tension remains: "I bought the beautiful baskets and prepared the shelves. Now what? How will children know what to do with this? How should I show it to them? What will keep all these materials from being dumped out and messed up?" These questions are valid and important. Compelling Materials do not exist in a vacuum. This is where Explicit Presentation comes into play: teachers develop and use clear communication techniques to demonstrate how children might use materials and processes. As a result, the children become independent, creative, and confident.

THE SECOND INTENTION

Explicit Presentation

Teaching for Confidence and Competence

Isaac and Jesse are playing with lacing cards. They eagerly lace up all the cards, discovering how satisfying it is to join two or more cards together with multiple laces. They work quickly to use all the materials. Once they have used up all the laces and cards, Isaac looks at Jesse and says, "Hey, let's go play in blocks!" Jesse, says, "Yeah, let's go!" The children leave the lacing cards, still attached to each other, on the table and hurry off to the block area.

Isaac and Jesse had fun, but is anyone going to use these lacing cards now? When materials are left this way, they often just stay a mess on the table until clean up time, when a teacher scoops them up and puts them away to deal with later. No child wants to come over and undo all those lacing cards in order to play with them. Unless children are explicitly taught how to get the materials they have been

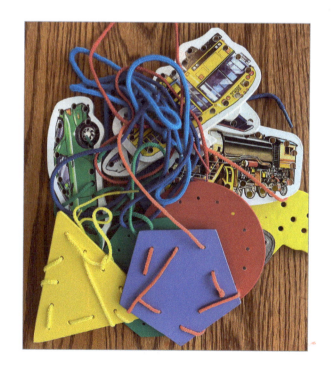

using ready for the next person, they will leave trails of materials all around the classroom, and teachers will shift into the "busy server" mode, cleaning up after everyone. ***In Complementary Curriculum, the intention of Explicit Presentation develops practices to teach children what you want them to know and be able to do successfully on their own.*** Without Explicit Presentations about how to use materials, care for them, and ready them for other children, classrooms become overrun with abandoned materials and activities.

Explicit Presentation refers to the practice of modeling everyday routines, activities, and the use of classroom materials, through descriptive language and non-verbal cues. It happens in small moments, such as when a teacher shows a child the process of how to care for and use a toy or material, how to carry a baby doll in the dramatic play area, how to put the caps back on markers, or how to take blocks off the shelf, build with them, and put them away again.

Explicit Presentation also happens more formally when a teacher gathers a group of children to offer them a lesson about the entire cycle of an activity: how to take the pegboard off the shelf, carry it to a table, carefully choose pegs from the basket to put on the board, then remove them and put them back in the basket, and return the pegboard to the shelf where it lives. For young children, there is no lesson too small: how to open a lunch box, put on a jacket, how to politely interrupt, or how to use a paintbrush. All of these activities require intentional instruction, because children will not simply discover these skills on their own. Even how to work with loose parts and open-ended materials requires some kind of introduction. Children learn how to carry materials from a shelf to a table and back, how to remove materials from containers (picture children dumping materials from great heights onto the floor), how to treat materials with care during exploration and discovery, and how to put them away so they are ready for the next person.

You may be thinking, *"But aren't we supposed to let children explore and discover things on their own?"* Yes, open-ended discovery must be balance with Explicit Presentations; it is not an either-or situation. Modeling by teachers does not thwart children's discovery. Instead, it supports children's ability to use materials more skillfully and for their own creative pursuits and discoveries. The teacher acts as a supportive guide, helping children engage with materials in ways that are meaningful to them (Standing, 1969). When children master specific techniques and strategies, they develop the competence and confidence to take risks and use materials in new ways. ***Explicit Presentation does not take the place of free exploration and discovery—it prepares children for it.***

Setting the Stage

There are four foundational practices that create a context for Explicit Presentations:

1. Prepare the Environment - Get What You Need
2. Prepare Your Voice - Tone and Talk
3. Prepare Your Body - Slow Down
4. Prepare the Children - Take it Out and Put it Away

Prepare the Environment: Get What You Need

Think about where you will give the presentation you have in mind. Do the materials lend themselves to playing on the floor or is a table the best surface? Will children be in chairs or kneeling on the floor? Will you be across from the child or right beside them? Make sure you know where your materials are and that you have everything you need.

We recommend using a mat for your formal Explicit Presentations to large and small groups. The mat

Intentionally teach how to carry a mat, unroll and roll it, and use it under an activity.

defines the space around the materials you will be sharing and draws attention to them. A small, low table can also work for some demonstrations. The mat or table helps to define the space so children can really focus on what you are showing them. Neutral solid colored mats or large carpet samples (roughly 2' by 3' in size) make a brightly colored, themed rug less busy for your presentations.

Prepare Your Voice: Tone and Talk

While it is important to foster back and forth exchanges with children and make inquiries as they play, minimal and carefully chosen language during Explicit Presentation allows children to focus on your movements and steps. Maria Montessori wrote about teacher voice, tone, and language during presentations, noting that when offering coaching or instruction, teachers should prioritize the key words and sometimes utilize silence, so children can focus on the main points of your demonstration, follow your hand movements, placement of objects, and the sequence of the activity.

Here are some key principles for giving Explicit Presentations. Present with enthusiasm, as if the lesson is the most special thing you will ever show a child. Challenge yourself to find joy in your presentation and work to empower your children to follow their interests, take risks with new materials, treat materials with care, and experience success in learning. Here is some specific guidance.

- **Volume**: Keep the volume of your voice low, or even try whispering, to draw children's attention to the presentation and to create curiosity about it. Did you ever lose your voice and notice that the noise level in your room dropped significantly when you couldn't talk? Communicating

with gestures and meaningful gazes can be just as effective as a loud voice. A soft voice also supports children for whom a sharp or loud voice can be triggering, thus raising their cortisol levels and feelings of stress. Try simply saying, "I have something new to show you today." As you slowly reveal a set of lacing cards, introduce them in a whisper: "These are lacing cards! I will show you how to use them—watch carefully."

@ snack?

- **Tone**: Communicate in a way that sends children the message that you want to share a meaningful experience with them. You want to communicate authority, safety, and a willingness to interact. There is an art to this. The tone should always be kind and respectful, even when you are redirecting and reminding. Children with trauma often have strong reactions to sharp tones and loud voices. Your voice should harness children's attention, not put them on edge or make them feel anxious.

- **Quality of Words**: When giving an Explicit Presentation, the words you use matter. Think about the words that will most succinctly and meaningfully communicate important aspects of the materials or process you want to demonstrate. For example: "The dots on the dice tell you how many jewels to choose." This phrase uses specific language that communicates how the game works and what a child needs to look for and do to play the game. These few words tell children the purpose of the dice and that there will be a counting aspect to the game. When a teacher says, "The alphabet cards across the top of the table tell us where to put the pictures that begin with those sounds," she tells the children that there will be some sorting involved and that they can look for symbolic cues to place the pictures.

- **Economy of Words:** A mantra for Explicit Presentation is: *"Show more than you tell and less is more!"* Try to use just the words you need to communicate the big ideas about the activity or process so that children can digest the key elements of your presentation. This means that, as you think about the *quality* of your words, you also think about the *quantity*. Young children, and many adults for that matter, can become overwhelmed when there is too much language to digest. Children, especially dual language learners, need thoughtful exposure to new language and clear, concise introductions to specific vocabulary. They also benefit from seeing things more than once, with key language added gradually. Sometimes this means simply showing something without words first, and then presenting it again with minimal language. For example, you might first demonstrate how to use a glue stick by simply saying, "This is a glue stick," and then using it to glue a small triangle on a piece of paper without talking about what you are doing. Then demonstrate it again, saying things like "cap off" and "twist, twist" to illuminate some key steps.

Prepare Your Body and Mind: Slow Down

Children are wonderful imitators. They watch us intently and then try out what we do. Have you observed children in dramatic play and heard a version of your voice coming out of their mouths or seen your movements replicated? Montessori referred to children's ability to take in information as the "absorbent mind." She noticed that, after observing a teacher or another child, young children understood how to use a material. This came with a caveat: Montessori pointed out that children's ability to make the movements and language of a presentation their own depended upon the deliberateness of the adult presentation. Fast presentations with

EXPLICIT PRESENTATION

lots of language can lead to less internalization of the process for the child, making imitation more challenging.

When you give an Explicit Presentation, your movements will need to be slower and more deliberate than you may be used to. While it may initially feel like you are unnaturally slow, think of this way of presenting as a mindfulness experience for both you and the children. Slow and deliberate attention to movement and language brings intention and joy to your work as you maintain an awareness of the materials and how children will use them. Here are a few ideas to help you work more slowly.

- **Plan it out**: Make notes or even a short script so you know ahead of time what you will say and do. Sometimes an activity has a fully developed lesson plan; use the lesson plan so that you can be deliberate in your words and actions.

- **Practice**: Try out the presentation in advance so that the actual presentation will go according to plan. You may find there are aspects of the presentation that do not work or need modification. With a little practice or rehearsing, you will feel more confident and able to present with a slow, calm pace that children can easily follow.

- **Points of Interest**: Think about what aspects of the materials and the process will really draw in children's attention. Maybe it is the shape of a stencil: take a few seconds to trace your finger around the stencil as you show it, accentuating the shape. Or our familiar glue stick: hold it beside your ear and listen for the 'pop' the lid makes when it is on tight. Use dramatic pauses and point out special aspects of the work.

Give presentations on how to use the area, gathering a small group and demonstrating use and clean up of an area and its items.

Prepare the Children:
Take It Out and Put It Away

Helping children see and experience the entire cycle of an activity or material helps them internalize how to use a material for their own pursuits and projects, take care of materials, and feel a sense of competence with materials—even ownership of them. This offers children agency, an important aspect of development that leads to self-directed learning and discovery. This is important whether the activity or materials lend themselves to open-ended experiences or have a more prescribed beginning, middle, and end. For example, with something open-ended like small wooden blocks, you might show how to carry the blocks from the shelf to the table, model some ways to use the blocks (stacking them, arranging them in pathways, and creating patterns with their colors or shapes) and then show how to pack the blocks up and put them back on the shelf. The emphasis is on the process of use, not prescribing what to build.

magnetic tiles? on light table?

An activity like squeezing orange juice has a defined beginning, middle, and end, with several key steps. In an Explicit Presentation, you would demonstrate those steps, in order, and then invite the children to try. How much of the process you demonstrate during Explicit Presentation depends on the type of material or activity. In all cases, showing children where materials live in the classroom, how to carry them to a play space, and how to put things away is crucial to children's success and cultivates a classroom community that takes care of materials and each other.

In addition to using Explicit Presentation to help children learn how to use new materials, you can use it to demonstrate how to care for materials and the room. There are games you can play with children in large or small groups to support the idea that there is "a place for everything and everything goes in its place."

Gather children in a circle, and unroll two mats in the center. Then choose a material for each mat, asking the children to watch you carefully as you walk to the shelf to get the materials to "see where each thing lives in the classroom." Then say, "Let's pretend I am all finished with this puzzle and I've gotten it ready for the next person by putting the pieces on the tray," or "I had fun with these lacing cards, and took the laces out of the holes, so now they are ready for another friend to play with." Then ask, "Who thinks they know where this puzzle goes on the shelf?" "Who would like to roll up a mat?" Ask a few children to take a turn carrying a material to its place on the shelf or rolling up a mat. This helps children see the process of getting a mat, choosing a material, and putting it away.

The Art of Explicit Presentation

From these foundations, you can begin using this simple structure for Explicit Presentation to present almost anything! Presentations can happen in a group or one-on-one. The following presentation structure may be used with an individual child or very small group, and it can be applied to a variety of materials and situations. The structure provides consistency and invites a teacher and a child into a conversation around a material or activity.

1. Invite the child(ren): "I have something new to show you today." "I would love to invite you to try something interesting today."

2. Show the child(ren) where the materials are located. "It is right over here on this shelf."

3. Arrange the material on a mat or table, to create a specific workspace. "Let's get a mat so we can work with this material." "Let's carry this carefully to the table."

4. Name the material: "This is called gem sorting." "These are called Unifix® cubes." "This is carrot cutting."

5. Begin the presentation. Invite the child(ren) to participate if appropriate.

6. Present the full cycle of presentation. Include the clean-up and returning the material to the shelf.

7. Hand off: Invite the child(ren) to do the activity themselves.

8. Check back while the children are playing to see if they need support and to admire their work with them.

9. Present aspects of the process again if the children need more coaching.

10. Support children as they clean up the material.

How and When to Present

The beauty of Explicit Presentations is that you can give them anywhere and at any time; the early childhood day is full of opportunities. There are three groupings to consider: presenting a lesson to individual children, to a small group, or to the whole group.

Explicit Presentation for Individual Children

Presenting to an individual child can be a spontaneous activity or something you plan for ahead of time, when a child is ready for something new. For example, as part of your math curriculum, you want to support children to move from sorting loose parts

After a teacher modeled plant care, this child was able to independently dust the leaves of classroom plants.

into little collections to counting their collections and then using numerical symbols to capture their counting. You consider which children are ready for this next step and make a note in your plan book that during the coming week you will offer this next step to four or five children. In your storage area, you have buttons for sorting and number cards that you prepare to add to the math area, and you plan an Explicit Presentation that you will share with individual children during choice time. When the time comes, you say to one child, "I have something new to show you today." Guiding the child to the math shelf, you show her the new tray of buttons and the basket of numeral cards. She helps carry the materials to a table, where you give an Explicit Presentation about laying the number cards on the table, then counting buttons into piles that match the numbers. Then, you offer the child the opportunity to play with the buttons and number cards.

You can offer the same materials spontaneously during choice time. You notice a child wandering through the room, a bit at loose ends; you know that he enjoys sorting games. You simply invite him in the moment: "You look like you are looking for something to do. I have something new to show you in the math area. Let's go check it out!" Or you notice that a child has been sorting the collections on the math shelf over the last few days, and is now starting to count the objects in the small groups she creates. The next time she works with the buttons, you sit down at her table and offer, "I have something new to show you with these buttons." You get a set of numeral cards and begin carefully placing them at the top of the table, saying, "The number tells us how many buttons to put under it. Let's count." You show the child how to count buttons to illustrate each number, creating a line of buttons under each numeral. You and the child play together for a while. Then you let her know how to clean up when she's done, and you leave her to this new game. These lessons allow you to move in and out of children's experiences as a supportive guide: "I'll be right back to see what this looks like when you are finished, and to help clean-up."

Explicit Presentation for Small Groups of Children

As with Explicit Presentation for an individual child, you can intentionally convene a small group of children to support their learning, or you can spontaneously jump into a group. For example, you know that there are three children who have mastered pouring liquid from a pitcher at the water table and are ready for more complex tasks with longer steps, such as watering plants in the classroom or serving snack to their friends. You note this in your plan book, so you can prepare an Explicit Presentation for these children during choice time to demonstrate plant care.

Spontaneous small groups can also occur during choice time. You see a child painting with watercolors, with three other children watching her—a great opportunity to have these children come together around their common interest in painting. You get three more paint sets, brushes, water cups, and art mats, saying, "I think all of you artists would like to work with watercolors. Let's make room at the table and I will give you all a lesson on how to use these paints. Let's gather round!"

You can take small groups into areas of the room to demonstrate the materials there. For example, you might gather a small group of children in the block area and say, "This is the block area, with small, medium, and really big blocks. This is how you carry the longest blocks." Model how to remove a long block from the shelf with a hand on each end, and how to gently place it on the rug, then ask, "Who would like to try?" Once there is a collection of blocks on the rug, you can model how to build a small structure with a few blocks. Then you can demonstrate how to clean-up, saying, "Now I am finished building. Watch how I put the blocks back so other friends can use them." If you know that children are interested in babies and you want to put some dolls in dramatic play, gather a small group of children to introduce the baby dolls, model how to carry them, and even how to pass a doll from child to child. Demonstrate how to change a diaper on the doll and put on her clothing. Begin to think ahead to the coming days and how you will add to children's skills with the baby dolls with an Explicit Presentation on washing the dolls in the sensory table.

The line between pre-planned and spontaneous can be a bit blurry, so allow yourself to both plan ahead and respond in the moment. Sometimes spontaneous presentations become plans for another child or group of children. Planned spontaneity is something to strive for so that you respond to children's needs in the moment and use your interactions to plan future learning experiences. You always want to have some materials and experiences ready and know who you might share them with, should the opportunity arise.

above some toddlers?

Explicit Presentation for Your Whole Group of Children

This is probably the most familiar and common way that teachers think of giving an Explicit Presentation. Many teachers gather children daily for a morning meeting or circle time, give one lesson to everyone, and check it off their list. In some classrooms, children come in and go right to choice time, in which case gathering a whole group can happen later in the day. In large groups, not every child may absorb your presentation, and you will need to make additional Explicit Presentations to individuals or small groups later. Also, the lesson you want to offer during a big group time, especially in mixed-age groups, may not be relevant for all the children. It may be more appropriate to offer intentional lessons tailored to the needs of a particular child or small group. When you decide that an Explicit Presentation to the whole group is best, get your mat or small table and your notes, and present away! Sometimes you will present something by yourself. Other times, you might want to have a co-teacher, assistant, or even a willing child co-present with you. For example, your co-teacher can play the role of a child. Or a child can model what it is like to receive a lesson and then carry out that activity herself.

Re-Presentations

By "re-presentation" we mean presenting something again. Children may need multiple presentations of routines and activities. Think about your own learning. Sometimes you need to see a process a few times before you feel really confident with it. Children are the same. Re-presentations can be pre-planned or spontaneous and are not an indication of any deficit within that child or group, but simply part of the developmental process of learning.

Categories of Presentations

Thinking about presentations by categories helps you to plan out what you will present over the course of a week, month, and year. Some lessons set the tone and foundation for developing a classroom community; they are especially important during the first days of a new school year, when you are integrating new children into a group, or when children move from one group to another. Other presentations support children's self-care and independence over time, promoting competence and confidence. Still other presentations are directly linked to specific content areas and the materials and processes associated with them. There are many types of Explicit Presentations that are specific to early childhood settings. The following foundational categories will inspire you to think about your own routines and the children and families in your program.

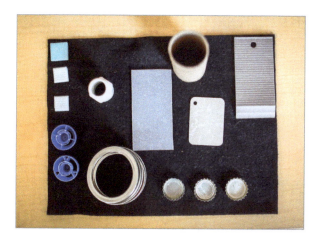

Fundamental Foundational Presentations

- **Getting from Here to There**: This involves helping children carry things such as trays, baskets, a chair, or a mat, and walking carefully around the room, taking things off shelves and putting them away. Look around your classroom: how do children use the space? What skills will help them move more fluidly through the room? What skills will help maintain physical order?

- **Loose Parts and Open-Ended Materials**: To orient children to the materials in the classroom, introduce them to what is on the shelves. Make a plan for when you will make these presentations. How will you pace the introduction of materials so children's sense of what is available expands over time?

- **Common Materials**: Classroom staples like crayons, markers, scissors, and glue sticks need introductions that include use and care of these items. Think about the order of how you will make these available and introduce them. Make a list of the materials you want children to have access to and learn to use, and plan a trajectory of when you will introduce them to children.

- **During Dramatic Play**: Children benefit from presentations on materials in the block area, dollhouse, and dramatic play area. Children will need instruction on how to use and care for the materials in these areas so they can use them successfully.

- **Care of Self and Environment:** Think of all the practical things it would be wonderful for children to be able to do independently and how that would support the settled classroom. For example, it is helpful for children to know how to put on gloves and mittens, a daily occurrence in places where the weather turns cold!

We encourage you to put the names of these "lessons" right into your plan book or planning template for the week or month so you have a sense of when you aim to present and whether you will present to an individual child, a small group, or the whole group. Write out lessons that are new for you, using these templates to support your planning.

Care of Self

- Putting on a coat: zippering, buttoning, snapping, fastening velcro
- Hanging up one's things in a cubby
- Opening a lunchbox and setting out food
- Using a tissue
- Putting on and taking off shoes
- Putting on and taking off gloves, mittens, socks
- Using the bathroom
- Handwashing
- Tooth brushing

Care of Others

- Serving food to other people
- Admiring someone's work
- Offering feedback to someone
- Helping a friend with a task
- Passing materials to a friend
- Offering help

Social Interactions

- Saying excuse me
- Moving past someone
- Holding a door open for another person
- Asking someone to pass you something
- Greeting visitors
- Leaving enough space between people at group meetings
- Asking for help

Care of the Environment

- Carrying materials
- Using materials
- Putting away materials
- Rolling up a rug
- Pushing chairs in at the table, and carrying chairs from one table to another
- Sweeping, and using dustpans
- Using a sponge to clean up a spill
- Dusting
- Washing a window
- Flower arranging
- Table setting
- Mopping or using a carpet sweeper

Conclusion:
Incorporating Presentations

If it is new to you, Explicit Presentation may initially feel a bit prescribed, technical, or even mechanical. But once you master it, it will become a natural aspect of your teaching and will even bring you joy. The joy comes from feeling confident in your teaching practice and knowing your children well enough to plan thoughtfully for their experiences. Designing interesting Compelling Materials and understanding how to engage in Explicit Presentations are integral aspects of a rich and rewarding professional life.

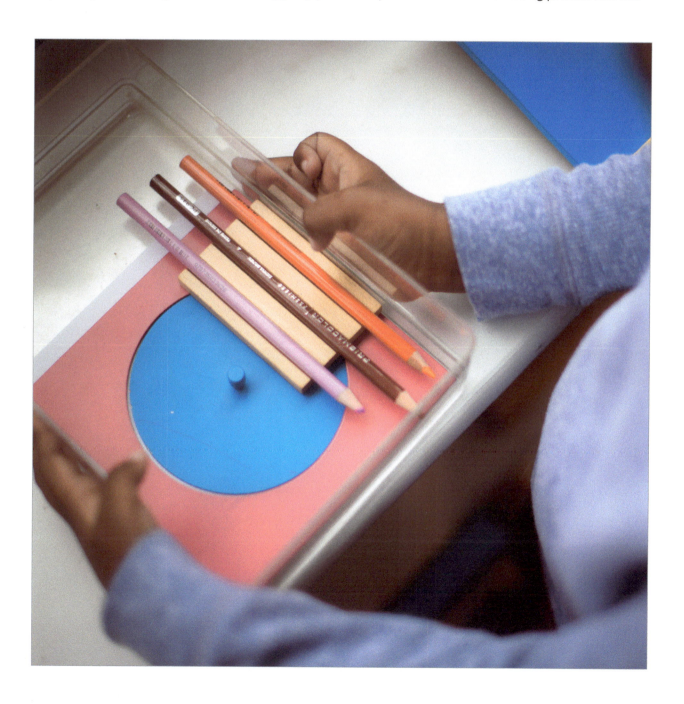

THE THIRD INTENTION

Responsive Scaffolding

Observing children as they discover new possibilities and supporting them in leaps of understanding and awareness

Joshua, who is two and a half, chooses a basket of Bristle Blocks® from the shelf. He grasps the basket with one hand, realizes it is too heavy, and isn't sure how to get it from the shelf to the floor. The teacher quietly moves next to Joshua, guides his hands to each side of the basket so that his thumbs are on top of the basket's edge and he's got a good grip, and then points him in the direction of the rug. Joshua successfully manages the weight of the basket as he carries the Bristle Blocks® through the classroom to the rug. He smiles to himself, pleased with his success. The teacher watches as he joyfully begins building.

Being an early educator is grounded in the joy of observing children as they discover new possibilities and supporting them in leaps of understanding and awareness. The third intention of the Complementary Curriculum Approach, Responsive Scaffolding, focuses on the windows of opportunity to enter children's experiences and support new learning. Responsive Scaffolding asks educators to observe children's play and interactions with materials in order to learn what they are trying to understand and what kinds of challenges they are looking for next. It refers specifically to the ways teachers move in and out of children's play, offering coaching and strategies for children to use as they develop skills and knowledge. This coaching, or scaffolding, grows from and strengthens trusting relationships between children and teachers.

Responsive Scaffolding requires you to observe and listen to children, so that you come to know them deeply. You need to know what intrigues them, what stymies them, what they care about, and how they think. Building on this intimate knowledge of a child's

Close listening is essential to Responsive Scaffolding. Take time to stop, look, and listen when children spontaneously share. When you ask a question, really listen to the child's answer.

thinking and playing, a teacher offers side-by-side coaching to support a child to master new learning and gain competence. Responsive Scaffolding asks teachers to step in close to offer coaching, and then to step back so a child can experience the pleasure of concentration and the gratification of "I did it myself!" Teachers offer Responsive Scaffolding throughout the day and across the learning environment as they support children's explorations of challenging and interesting materials, social interactions, and daily routines. Responsive Scaffolding is a strategy that helps children become more independent and confident learners.

Scaffolding as a Foundation for Learning

We cannot talk about scaffolding without acknowledging the work of psychologist and development theoretician Lev Vygotsky, who focused much of his work on how we learn, the conditions that support learning, and the role of relationships in learning. An integral part of the learning process, as Vygotsky saw it, involves what he called *scaffolding*: the coaching that happens in a person's Zone of Proximal Development, or ZPD. The Zone of Proximal Development is the space between what a learner can do on their own and what a learner can eventually do with support. Vygotsky explained that when

Responsive Scaffolding is a mutual activity. Notice the child giving direction to the teacher who is representing the child's ideas about how to get the rocket ship to stay on the side of the loft. The teacher is helping and the child is leading.

a child at one level of competence is exposed to a peer or adult's modeling of the next level of skill or know-how, they can gradually reach a new level of "independent performance," or new competence. He believed that educators support a child's learning by understanding their Zone of Proximal Development and offering just the right amount of challenge to help a child stretch into new capacities.

The keys to understanding a child's ZPD are observation and listening. By watching a child as she interacts with materials, tries new activities, and works with peers, you will learn about her strengths and weaknesses. You may notice which kinds of puzzles in the classroom are too easy for her and which are too hard, how she uses blocks and where she gets stuck in her construction, and where she stumbles and flourishes in her collaborative dramatic play. Getting to know a child means really spending time with her, getting to know what kinds of books she enjoys, what kinds of materials she prefers, and how she interacts with her peers. Children give teachers many opportunities to get to know them; it is just a matter of spending time and being observant.

Vygotsky believed that if children are left to discover things only on their own, their abilities might not progress, since learning grows from exposure to and experience with meaningful activities alongside a supportive teacher or peer. This is very different from thinking that it is not possible for children to advance in their learning until certain developmental stages are in place. For example, thinking that a child will not be able to complete a more challenging activity until his brain and fine motor control are at a specific developmental point actually deprives children of learning experiences. Vygotsky encourages teachers to invite a child to stretch.

While a child's developmental trajectory may determine when things are introduced (we don't try to teach babies to tie their shoes), experiences should not be withheld because a child had been deemed "not ready." From this perspective, readiness is about seeing every child as primed for exposure. When children are offered a range of learning opportunities, what they can do independently and what they can do with support becomes clear. Then a teacher can adjust offerings based on what they observe. Look for windows of opportunity that show that a child is ready for a stretch into new learning.

Teachers scaffold children's learning in many ways, from how teachers prepare the environment to the small prompts and supports they offer and Explicit Presentations they make (Bedrova and Leong, 2007). Scaffolding is built on the foundation of relationships—teachers knowing children well and understanding their curiosities and capacities. Teachers who are deeply connected to the children, their strengths and areas for growth, and their interests and abilities, can provide support to all learners.

The intention of Explicit Presentation was introduced in the previous chapter. Responsive Scaffolding and Explicit Presentation share a commitment to supporting children's success in the learning process through direct offerings by teachers, using deliberate movements, intentional language, and a thoughtfully modulated voice and tone. The moves you make during an Explicit Presentation, and later as a child engages with a material, are scaffolds to support success. After you read this chapter, you may want to go back and reread Explicit Presentation through the lens of Responsive Scaffolding. It will give Explicit Presentation a whole new meaning!

Teacher scaffolding helps children and adults slow down before embarking on an activity. Here, the teacher took time to ask the children what they noticed, in detail, before they began drawing. By paying close attention to the material and including important details, they created more satisfying representations of the flower.

Supporting Children through Scaffolding

Responsive Scaffolding contributes to children's well-being. Studies have shown that scaffolding children's learning reduces stress, helps them sustain focus, and helps children internalize their own possibilities for independence, competence, and self-regulation (Bedrova and Leong, 2007). Consider children's stress level during the learning process. When tasks are consistently too challenging or overwhelming, a child can get very frustrated, especially if they repeatedly experience failure and a lack of completion. Educators can reduce children's stress through Responsive Scaffolding by finding a "just right" balance of challenge *and* success.

Imagine you have a child who keeps trying to use small LEGO® pieces, but who has a hard time fitting the blocks together; the LEGO® bricks keep falling apart, and the child never gets very far in her building. She tries and tries, and keeps failing. Eventually, the child gives up on LEGOS®, mad, sad, and disappointed. **Responsive Scaffolding offers a different ending to this story!** Imagine that the child's teacher observes her difficulty with the LEGOS® and says, "I am noticing those blocks are really tricky for you. Would you like to try a different kind of block? I think a bigger size would work better for you." The teacher offers the bulkier DUPLOS™ blocks and encourages the child to give them a try. When the child presses two DUPLO™ bricks together, they lock together—success! And off she goes, building successfully and with pleasure. The teacher's Responsive Scaffolding helped the child navigate her way out of the stress of failure. Look for opportunities like this to bring children joy and peace in ways that are a "good fit" for where they are cognitively and emotionally.

RESPONSIVE SCAFFOLDING

Responsive Scaffolding helps children sustain focus as they play and work. When children experience the satisfaction and creativity that come with using materials for their own pursuits, they are more likely to stay interested and stick with a project—cultivating perseverance, persistence, and grit. For example, a child is trying to use an eye-dropper to suck colored water out of a jar and squeeze it onto a piece of absorbent paper, but she cannot quite master how to squeeze the top just right to suck in the liquid. Her teacher watches for a few moments to understand what is not working for the child, admiring her willingness to keep trying but aware that she might soon become too frustrated and give up. Once the teacher has an idea of what the child needs to know about the eyedropper, she steps in to demonstrate how to squeeze the rubber top and release it before lifting it from the jar, explaining how to use the eyedropper as she demonstrates. Then, she suggests that the child try, offering to hold the eyedropper with her so they can move through the process together. With this scaffolding, the teacher encourages the child's "stick-to-itiveness," a mindset that helps children concentrate, work through problems, and experience the satisfaction that comes with seeing a project through to the end, even when it is challenging. Children thrive when they have the time and support to hunker down with a task, game, or creative project and follow it through to a satisfying completion.

When children experience repeated success, their self-esteem grows. Children, indeed, all of us, want to feel successful and capable. Interesting, fun, joyful play creates the conditions that promote children's sense of themselves as people who can successfully take on projects that matter to them. When they navigate the challenges, aha moments, and discoveries that come with any meaningful pursuit, children develop trust in their competence and a feeling that "I can do it!" For example, consider the common situation of classroom spills, both dry and wet, on floors, tables, and at easels. When a spill happens, a teacher can use Responsive Scaffolding to support

These friends are engaged in peer scaffolding as an older child instructs a younger child, step by step.

the child, saying, "When the water spills out of the water table, we can wipe it up with a sponge so that the floor doesn't get slippery. Have you tried that before? Let me show you what I know about how to use a sponge to get water off the floor."

In the following example, look for the ways Ben experiences stress, regains focus, and experiences success, and how Responsive Scaffolding supports him.

Ben slams a puzzle piece down on the surface of the table and covers his face with his hands. The teacher asks, "Ben, are you okay?" Ben doesn't answer. The teacher moves over to Ben and sits next to him. "This puzzle has a lot of pieces. It can feel confusing! I wonder if that's what you're feeling. One thing that I know about puzzles like this is that it helps to make the edge first, then the rest will be a bit easier." Slowly and with intention, the teacher begins to sort the edge pieces to the bottom of the table, pointing to their straight sides. The teacher explains, "These are called the edge pieces. They make the outside edges of the puzzle, like making a frame. Let's find those pieces. Can you help me?" Ben begins to search for and find them with her. The teacher connects a few edge pieces, asking Ben, "Can you find a piece that attaches to mine?" As Ben becomes more confident, the teacher says, "Ben, you are doing so well. I am going to help another child and then check back on you." Ben works on the puzzle throughout choice time, beaming as he connects piece after piece. Eventually, he's able to complete the frame of the puzzle, mostly on his own.

There is another important aspect of how Responsive Scaffolding supports children's well-being at work in this story—constructive support for children's behavior. Teachers often think about behavior management as something to do when a child loses control, gets into a conflict, or exhibits aggressive or anti-social behavior. Rather than seeing behavior management as solely a corrective response to behavior you want to squelch, it can be reframed as offering children support before their behavior frays.

Ben's teacher noticed that Ben was becoming frustrated with the puzzle. Her first response could have been corrective: "Ben, we don't slam the puzzle pieces." Instead, she acknowledged Ben's frustration, the feeling "inside" his angry slam, giving him language for his feelings and honoring his experience. She then offered some specific scaffolding to address the aspect of the situation that was frustrating him. She addressed the task, not the child. She didn't think that the puzzle itself was too difficult for Ben because she had seen him complete other similar puzzles, but this one had a few more pieces than previous puzzles and Ben needed some new strategies. Her scaffolding supported Ben to put the puzzle together with pride and warded off a possible tantrum. This is behavior management at its best. As you observe children's play, ask yourself, "What support does this child need from me to move through frustration into success?" When teachers do this, their classrooms can become happier and more understanding spaces.

Explicit Presentation is a key component of Responsive Scaffolding. Initial and ongoing presentations support children's success and confidence with materials.

As Ben has more practice and time with puzzles, he will need less and less support and will be able to complete puzzles like this one independently. This is a great example of the difference between being primed for exposure and developmental readiness. No amount of assistance will support success if you give a toddler a 100-piece puzzle; that would be a set-up for failure. But Ben's 20-piece puzzle was within reach for him, with some empathic coaching from his teacher. Being sure that the scope and design of materials are within range for a child addresses developmental readiness. Know each child's skill set with materials so you know when they are ready to jump to a new level of competence and independence.

Everyday Responsive Scaffolding Strategies in the Classroom

Complementary Curriculum Approach offers five everyday strategies that you can use to implement Responsive Scaffolding. Although teachers who have worked in classrooms for years might already use these techniques, even so it will be helpful to recognize, name, and unpack these exchanges with children.

Strategy 1: Allow a Gradual Release

A crucial part of scaffolding children's learning is eventually creating distance between the teacher and child so the child can fully engage in the experience at a level of independent performance. When a teacher uses the strategy of "gradual release," she helps children get started on an activity and underway with a trajectory. Then she checks back in with less and less frequency as the child carries on with the activity. For example, it can be tricky for a child who is learning how to use paints to figure out how to get the excess paint off the brush, before starting to paint. A teacher may decide to offer Responsive Scaffolding. She sees that the child already knows how to dip the brush into a cup of paint and swirl it around to load it up with paint, so she builds on that by saying, "Let me show you this next step. It will help you get the brush ready to use for painting, so it doesn't drip paint on your paper where you don't want it." The teacher demonstrates how to run the brush against the edge of the paint cup to reduce the volume of paint on the brush, then lifts the brush out of the cup and points out that it's not dripping paint. She hands the brush to the child, inviting him to try, and offers a bit of coaching as he gives it a go. As he begins to paint on his own again, the teacher stays nearby for a moment, in case he could use further coaching. She is not hovering, but available—and in a moment she steps back, completing the scaffolding experience.

Consider a child who is just learning how to pump on a swing. At first, the child will need lots of help to figure out how to push her legs out and then fold them back at the right times. The teacher thinks about who she knows this child to be, how the child learns best, and what strategies she might offer. She knows that this child loves to give high fives every morning upon arrival at school, and that gives the teacher an idea. She says, "Let's try this! I will put my hands up and I want you to try to give them high fives with your feet!" Exuberantly, the child extends her feet out to give the teacher's hands a double high five. The child's feet naturally fall back in a release after the high five, and the swing moves back, away from the teacher. High five after high five, the child moves her feet in and out, and the swing starts to climb higher. The teacher continues to offer high fives to get the child to pump forward. Slowly, as the child gains mastery of the pumping movement, the teacher offers less and less support until the child is pumping back and forth proudly on her own.

Observing and listening to children is the key to offering the right amount of support and knowing when and how to withdraw it. Every child's needs are different, and the timing and pace of gradual release is individual. It's important to know the children's signs of frustration, confusion, joy, and understanding. These cues guide you in knowing when to continue your coaching and when to step away.

Strategy 2: Engage in Activities Yourself

When children are playing, offer Responsive Scaffolding to help them find ways to move more deeply into their encounters with materials and each other. Teachers can do this by playing with materials themselves and talking out loud about what they are doing. When teachers demonstrate pleasure and interest and model the complexities of how they're using a material, they can spark children's curiosity and eagerness to try a material or activity in different or more complex ways.

The teacher noticed that the beading activity on the manipulatives shelf was not being used much. She wondered if it had run its course. She had also noticed that children hadn't done much beyond putting beads on the string, and she thought it might be time for them to see other possibilities for how to use the beads. During a peaceful time in the classroom, she carried the beading work from the shelf to an open seat at a table by the window. Modeling focus and engagement, the teacher deliberately strung one bead at a time in rainbow order, quietly saying, "Red, orange, yellow, green, blue..." A group of children gathered, curious about what she was doing. She narrated her work: "I am making a bracelet with a pattern." Once the beads were all strung, she carefully knotted the string to make a bracelet, and put it on her wrist. She exclaimed, "There! It's done. I love it!" She carried the rest of the beads and strings back to the shelf. Immediately afterwards, a child took the basket of beads off the shelf and gave beading a try.

When teachers demonstrate new possibilities for materials, the goal is not to have children mimic exactly what they do, but rather to see new ways of working with materials that may have challenges the children have not yet considered. The teacher in this example helped the children find new complexity and possibilities in the beads. When teachers do this, they reinvigorate their classrooms—and they get to play too!

Strategy 3: Be a Dramatic Play Stage Manager

Dramatic play is an important venue for children to take on roles, practice social interactions, use their imagination, represent their experiences, be silly, and be bigger than their usual selves. Vygotsky captured this when he said, "In play, a child is always above his average age, above his daily behavior; in play, it is as though he were a head taller than himself" (1967). Through dramatic play, children try on new ways of being that support their emotional, social, and cognitive development. When children become overwhelmed, which can spiral into acting out, adults can play a key role in creating a meaningful culture of dramatic play, serving as a sort of stage manager to scaffold children's experiences. This does not mean that a teacher takes over the children's pretend play or has to be in the dramatic play area all the time. Instead, a teacher engages in a series of high-level interactions, moving in and out of play, building and extending children's capacity for pretend play.

For example, children sometimes enter a dramatic play area unsure of what role to take on or how to join a pretend play scenario already in progress. To help children launch a scenario, a teacher can ask, "Who would you like to pretend to be?" If a few children are already in the dramatic play area with a scenario already in motion, a teacher can let newcomers know what the story line is about and who the children are pretending to be. You might say, "Come on in! Molly is pretending to be the daddy driving a car, Simon is pretending to be the family puppy, and Laura is the doctor coming to check in on the baby. Who do you want to be in this story?" Once the children have settled into the play together, you can slowly withdraw.

Some children may need even more direct scaffolding to be successful in dramatic play. A teacher can use children's literature to offer storylines and roles for pretend play. For example, in one classroom, the children had been reading and enjoying the story of the Three Little Pigs over the course of a few days. The teachers decided to provide a space in dramatic play for the children to explore this story. The teachers were hopeful that the children would have the opportunity to experience the story firsthand and retell it in their own way. They added props such as headbands with pig ears, bundles of hay, a basket of sticks, and some cardboard bricks. At first, a teacher sat at the side of the dramatic play area with the Three Little Pigs storybook and narrated the book for the children to act out. She suggested lines for the children to say and offered stage direction about how children could act out the building and huffing and puffing and falling down. As the children became more adept with roles and props, the teacher handed over the narrator role to a child, and started to remove herself from the dramatic play area. Gradually, the children started to tell their own versions of the Three Little Pigs and began to use the props in their own creative ways.

Strategy 4:
Invite Children to Coach Each Other

Just as children can learn from teachers, they can also learn from each other. Children have a range of abilities in a variety of areas that teachers can tap into. Children are highly capable of helping each other, pairing up to work together on a task where one child can learn from another. The opportunity to teach and learn from each other offers children the chance to be leaders and models, as well as co-constructors and collaborators, moving beyond their individual understandings of a concept or situation. It is important to make sure that children have the opportunity to be both teachers and learners in peer coaching; being aware of each child's strengths, teachers know when a child would be a great resource for their peers. Teachers can connect children to each other by suggesting, "Justin, you have had a lot of practice sewing; do you have a

minute to teach Emma about threading the needle?" "Julia, I remember how you built that block tower yesterday. Can you show Emre how to make a stable base for her castle?"

In this photo, Jeff is coaching Max about how to assemble a puzzle. Their teacher observed that Max was struggling with where to start the puzzle and asked him if he would like some help. She turned to Jeff, who had done this puzzle many times. "Jeff, would you be willing to show Max what you know about this puzzle? I've noticed that you've put it together a bunch of times." As they began, the teacher offered some coaching about how they might work together: "Max, what kind of help do you want?" "Jeff, can you explain to Max how you figure out where a piece goes?" Jeff, eager to show what he knew, jumped in with a suggestion to sort the pieces by color and to put corner pieces aside. He and Max worked together to frame the puzzle and then began filling in the rest of the pieces.

These moments are important because they provide children with the opportunity to be experts and collaborators, giving them a chance to notice what they know and make it visible to a friend and to themselves. When children share their thinking with each other, they are more than just kind helpers; they are guiding each other and creating a respectful community of learners.

Strategy 5:
Read Nonverbal Cues and
Respond with Nonverbal Supports

Sometimes the opportunity for scaffolding and the support you offer can be beautifully simple and not require any words at all. Some children are very expressive verbally, capable of asking for help when they need it. Others may cozy up to you or act out when they need support. It is important to know each child's cues so you can fully support their efforts. The opening description of a teacher gently supporting a child's hands to successfully carry a basket is an example of this kind of simple scaffolding.

Teachers encourage children to ask each other questions, such as: 'How did you build that?' 'What are you building?' and, 'Can you show me how?' Children internalize these questions and serve as resources for each other.

Here is another:

Two children, both almost three years old, are in the block area stacking blocks. They want to build something big, and talk excitedly about making a tower. They stack the blocks quickly and without much attention to the sizes of the blocks or the order in which the blocks are stacked. After growing to six blocks, the tower falls. This happens again and again. At first, the children laugh, but soon enough, they grow frustrated. One child begins to cry and the other throws a few blocks—not hard, but clearly indicating that the children are stuck. The teacher enters the block area, gathers the blocks, and motions to the children to sit with her. She begins building a new tower using small blocks of the same shape. After stacking three blocks, she silently passes a small block to one of the children and motions for her to put it on top of the tower, gently showing her how to adjust the block so it is stable. Then the teacher passes a block to the other child, pointing to the top of the tower. They continue this way for a few more turns, until the tower is about half the size of the children. Then, the teacher takes the children's hands, steps back with them to admire the tower, and begins to take down each block, offering the children a chance to rebuild it themselves.

Conclusion: Looking for Windows of Opportunity

If you are wondering when Responsive Scaffolding should happen, the answer is, "Always!" It can happen throughout the day and in any area of the classroom or playground. You attune yourself to each child's window of opportunity: those moments when a child is ready to count higher, mix more colors of paint, negotiate a challenging experience with a peer, or try to pump on the playground swing.

Responsive Scaffolding is not about what you are doing "for" or "to" children; it is about being an ally, a co-collaborator, a helper, and a facilitator. All of this is in the service of helping children feel proud, confident, and competent as they develop new skills, insight, and new levels of learning. It takes time for Responsive Scaffolding to become intuitive. As you really get to know the children in your classroom, their interests, personalities, and learning styles, you will learn how to best support every child.

THE FOURTH INTENTION

Following Children's Interests

Teachers and Children Learning Together

"My director told me that it was time to study polar bears simply because winter was coming. Right away we pulled out polar bear figures and white playdough and set them up on classroom tables. We also added ice with colorful spray bottles to the sensory table. The curriculum wasn't rooted in any kind of big idea or interest of the children, but rather was based on a "cute" activity the director found. Would the children like the activities? Perhaps. Would it have meaning and lead to deep learning over time? Probably not."

Following familiar curriculum themes using the same activities year after year makes planning easy, but can also become routine and uninteresting for teachers and for children. Often, pre-planned offerings are detached from children's lives, communities, and interests. Some teachers shared how they made a shift from routine themes to a more engaging way of teaching.

"We used to use the same content each year that followed the seasons. It became very stale and boring for everyone. The idea of observing children closely and then being inspired by their interests and our own interests has changed the fundamental way we think about what to bring into our classrooms. Today our classroom community approaches our curriculum topics with the excitement that can only come from deep curiosity and the desire to know more."

The fourth intention of Complementary Curriculum is Following Children's Interests. This is a core intention for a settled, responsive, engaged classroom because it is at the heart of educators' work. Children have new and inspiring ideas to share that teachers may have never considered before. Following Children's Interests supports mutual understanding between teachers and children. Teachers observe children's play and conversations and ask children what they already know and what they want to learn about. By following children's interests, teachers are less likely to succumb to a pitfall of thematic curriculum—short-term, adult-centered, irrelevant activities. A teacher's ability to know what children think, feel, and wonder is at the core of a settled, responsive, engaged classroom.

What does it really mean to follow children's interests? How can teachers provide experiences for children that are meaningful, joyful, and promote both communal and individual learning? Teachers are constantly trying to balance externally imposed curriculum goals and the emerging interests of children, simultaneously asking, "What do children want to know about?" and, "What do I want to make sure children know about?" Sometimes curriculum originates from children's ideas and play scenarios, or a spontaneous event in children's lives and community. Other times an educator may have a passion, an idea about something connected to children's lives, community, or even a mandated curriculum content area. This still requires close observation of play, talking with children about the content, and finding out what they know and want to know more about, before planning.

Learning from Emergent Curriculum and the Project Approach

Whether building curriculum on something that emerged initially from the children or on an idea that came from a teacher, working with Big Ideas helps shape and guide the direction you will take (Lesaux, Harris, & Duke, 2015). Big Ideas are overarching conceptual statements and questions about topics that inspire further inquiry. However, the curriculum they inspire does not live in a vacuum. This intention integrates thinking from Emergent Curriculum and the Project Approach, which hold two convictions in common: 1) children's interests are at the core of early childhood curriculum and 2) acting on what you know about these interests is at the heart of designing and offering materials, sharing presentations, and interacting with children. Emergent Curriculum and the Project Approach offer pathways for exploring Big Ideas. This chapter explores the strategy of Big Ideas and how to construct them with your children.

Big Ideas

A Big Idea is something that has meaning and relevance to your group and that grounds you and the children in an investigation. Rather than random activities about polar bears or holidays, a Big Idea inspires the topic that you decide to pursue with the children. A Big Idea matters to you and to the children; it intrigues you or challenges you. It is connected to a central aspect of your community's life, identity and being. Big Ideas should have the following components:

1. They are usually statements informed by children's questions, and they can be reframed as questions.

2. They should engage teachers and students, support sustained and deep knowledge building, and provoke thinking and more questions.

3. They should be relevant to children's interests and promote further inquiry in a range of content areas.

First, Big Ideas often take the form of statements about a topic or area of interest, often informed by children's questions. Figure 4 contrasts traditional themes that may last for only a day or week, with larger, more complex ideas that can be explored in depth over time. Sometimes, Big Ideas can be framed from children's questions and stated in the form of a big inquiry question. There are no hard and fast rules for which comes first, a Big Idea or children's questions. What is important is to stay open to the organic nature of this work.

Figure 4

Unit or Theme for Standard Practices	Unit or Theme for Advanced Instruction: The BIG IDEAS
Valentine's Day	• People care about each other. People can send messages to each other to share their feelings. • How do people show they care about each other?
Winter/Snow	• When the weather changes, we have to adjust. • What do animals do when the weather changes?
Cars/Transportation	• People need to go from one place to another. • How do people get from one place to another?
Dr. Martin Luther King Jr.'s Birthday	• What makes something fair? How can we include everyone?

For example, suppose the children in your program are playing pet store and pretending to be dogs, "talking" to each other by barking. This activity is lasting for days, and you observe the joy and commitment to this group game. In a small group meeting you decide to pose some questions: "How do animals talk to each other?" "What kinds of sounds do they make?" You bring in a video of dogs interacting with each other to watch with the children; you talk about it with them afterwards, asking the children what they noticed and what they wonder about. As you listen to children's observations, ideas, and questions, you begin to think about some large questions: "Do dogs have their own language?" or "How can we tell what dogs are saying?" Either of these questions could be reframed into a Big Idea about communication: "People and animals communicate in different ways." Or, "Dogs use actions and their voices to talk to each other. How is that the same and different from how we talk to each other?" Keep Big Ideas connected to children's questions and interests by continuing to observe and reflect on children's play and by posing and generating questions with children. As you build on children's natural curiosity and a desire to know more, you will adjust your curriculum plans, but the Big Idea will keep you grounded.

Second, Big Ideas should be engaging and should support sustained and deep knowledge building. This is different from superficial topical ideas, aimed at teaching predetermined content knowledge. At the beginning, the Big Idea might seem simple, but given time and attention, many possible avenues of exploration unfold, giving the work more depth and interest. Big Ideas should provoke thinking and give rise to more questions, rather than only moving in a straight line towards facts and informational learning. Big Ideas should be abstract enough to promote further inquiry and concrete enough to ground a study. To continue with the dog example, the Big Idea could be: "Animals communicate in different ways depending upon their abilities and where they live." Within this Big Idea is the flexibility to explore many things, while still anchored in how different animals in our world communicate. Children could study aquatic animal communication, terrestrial animal communication, or even subterranean animal communication. They might be interested in the different modes of vocalization that animals produce and the possible meanings of animal communication. This is different from a single, static topic such as "dogs," which could end up simply being a series of disconnected activities.

Finally, the Big Idea should be relevant to children's interests and support their curiosity about the world. Big Idea teaching and learning creates connections to children's experiences by bringing in every day opportunities that reflect their lives. Big Ideas bring relevance to learning. Because Big Ideas are applicable to children's lives, this approach facilitates deeper understanding of content knowledge as children are given the opportunity to learn real information.

For example, children exploring how clothes get clean might be interested in how a washing machine works, which could lead to experiences with force and motion, or how soap is made. Some experiences may be derived from your community, such as a visit to a laundromat. Many programs engage in a community or neighborhood unit and exploration every year, which is certainly worth doing, no matter your group of children. Using the Big Ideas approach, the children's interests would supply the focus for your areas of study. Here is an example. One teacher started her usual Community unit by asking children about people who were helpers in their large school building. It became clear that the children, while somewhat interested in the people in the building, were really fascinated with how the building was built and who made it.

This led to a two-month study of architecture, construction, and the design of the building, grounded in the Big Idea: Architects design buildings and other kinds of structures. Big Ideas can emerge from both predetermined conversations and random, spontaneous topics.

Emergent Curriculum

John Dewey advocated for curriculum to come directly from children's exploration, discoveries, and fascinations. He felt that education and learning are social and interactive processes. These ideas have come to be known as Emergent Curriculum and are one way to approach Big Idea work. In Emergent Curriculum teachers observe children's play, take up their ideas, and plan accordingly (Cassidy, Mims, Rucker, & Boone, 2003). The goal of Emergent Curriculum is for children and teachers to construct the curriculum together, thinking about ideas of substance that intrigue them, and discovering new understandings and questions that resonate for the group. This "co-construction" of curriculum is important because teachers and children develop mutual understandings when ideas and interests are shared. When you teach this way, children's

Each activity on this shelf is somehow related to bees, a topic children in this classroom had been studying.

motivation rises because the curriculum was created in partnership as opposed to solely imposed by the teacher. With Emergent Curriculum adults must observe children closely, listen to their dialogue, document their questions (either through writing notes or brainstorming as a group), design ways to foster interest, and then ask more questions.

In addition to topics suggested by children, a topic can arrive in your classroom from spontaneous events that result in a shared experience. For example, a bumblebee might fly into your room and buzz around, sparking interest and fear that is worth exploring. Or imagine that your students find an amazing eggshell on the playground. Where did the egg come from? How did it land on the playground? What bird was in there? Why isn't the egg in the nest now? Did the bird die? How long did the bird take to come out of the egg? Do different birds have different eggs? Capitalizing on spontaneous, shared experiences offers a rich opportunity for children and teachers to create curriculum together.

Emergent Curriculum does not necessarily have to end up being an in-depth project, but it could—depending on the direction a teacher wants to take with a child or group of children. Taking children's emerging interests into account is what makes the investigation vibrant and relevant for children and teachers. Emergent curriculum can be the initial seed of a long-term study, or Project Approach.

As part of a project on local workers, children go out into the community and help by cleaning their bus stop.

Project Approach

Project Approach offers another avenue for working with Big Ideas. The beauty of using Project Approach as an umbrella framework is that it gives you a scaffold and trajectory for your investigation and helps you to unfold the curriculum gradually over time in meaningful ways. Project Approach provides you with the steps to conduct a long-term, in-depth investigation, whether it is based purely on children's interests in something spontaneous or a topic that is more prescribed or predetermined. A project has a specific structure and arc, and it can last a week or two, a few months, or even unfold over the course of a year—morphing and evolving in new and interesting ways. It can support the study of topics that emerge initially from the children or adults, and it fosters the emergence of new directions and questions along the way. Curriculum topics, even if adult-determined, should incorporate an emergent lens.

There are many resources you can consult to learn more about the steps. *Picturing the Project Approach* outlines the process with clarity and simplicity (Kogan, Chard, & Castillo, 2017). The first step is to identify the project topic by engaging children in conversations about their prior experiences and using drawing, play, and discussion to share their knowledge. Part of this process is to help children raise questions about what they want to know more about. A second step is to prepare for fieldwork and either take children out into the community to visit sites and local experts or invite experts in. Working with children to represent their ideas, photographing the learning process and reflecting on it with children, and developing materials for children to engage with the topic across content areas, all support learning and development. Finally, you will want to prepare for the conclusion of the project and plan for how you might share the story of the project with families and the community at large. This can be done via photo essays, displays of children's work in the program space and in the community, celebrations with families, and children's summaries of what they learned.

Plan with Children's Interests in Mind

Whether inspired by Emergent Curriculum or Project Approach, close listening and intentional planning are the foundation for your Big Idea curriculum. You will need to identify children's interests and make choices about what to study with them. There are plenty of opportunities throughout the day for learning what children are thinking and wondering. This can happen on the playground, in the block area, or at the snack or lunch table. When you have conversations with colleagues about what you hear, you can think together about how to design your curriculum. Here are some planning strategies to support Following Children's Interests.

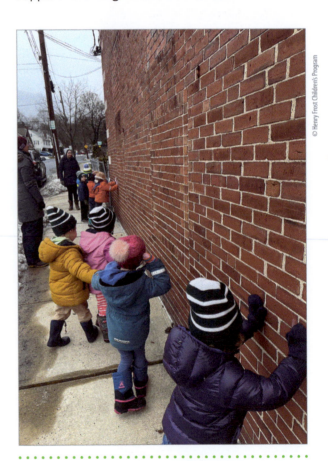

On the way back from their walk, children noticed a brick wall and pushed on it to see how strong bricks are!

Observing and Listening

Make time in your classroom to simply observe and listen to your students throughout the day. What are they talking about at snack or in the art area? What themes in their play do they repeatedly return to? Has a topic mentioned at circle time piqued their interest? What materials have been engaging to the class during choice time? What are they doing with the materials? It is helpful to take notes and photos so you can reflect on your experiences in the classroom.

With practice, you will get better and better at knowing which strands of children's interests to follow. For example, you might see your students repeatedly playing pet shop with the blocks in your classroom. When you ask children about their game they might be extremely excited to talk about the different animals in their pet shop and how they care for them. By observing and talking with your children, you can identify the topic, for example "People take care of pets to keep them healthy and loved."

Reflecting on Observations and Planning with Colleagues

Sit with your observation notes or your memories of children's interactions. Talk and think about what you heard and saw. Once you think you have landed on an idea children are interested in and have identified possible Big Ideas to explore, take some time to brainstorm with your colleagues and children. You can set the path for planning by (1) taking the time to reflect with teaching partners about what children might know and be interested in and (2) uncovering what you know and need to know about a topic. Make a list of resources you might need, and go back to the first intention, Compelling Materials, to begin designing some discrete work for children to choose that aligns with your topic of study.

Brainstorming with Children

Brainstorming with children can happen one-on-one or in small groups throughout the school day. Try asking open-ended questions such as: "I noticed that

As part of an investigation of architecture, children went on a walking field trip to draw nearby houses. They noticed things like rooflines, windows, and doors.

you were playing kitty family with Zoe this morning. Can you tell me more about that story and what you were doing?" Or, "This afternoon I watched you building that amazing structure and I heard you call it a skyscraper. Can you tell me more about your work?" Asking questions can define and hone in on exactly what your children are interested in and help you develop where to take the curriculum next.

Brainstorming can also be more formal and happen with the entire class at a meeting time. It is helpful to use some visual charting to help stimulate the children's contributions. There are wonderful tools and resources for eliciting children's ideas. An "inquiry web" maps adult and children's ideas about a topic and clarifies what children know and want to know.

In Figure 5, an example from a "heroes" study illustrates how teachers began to frame children's knowledge as a Big Idea: Heroes help animals every-day. Heroes help the planet earth. These kinds of webs support the process of surfacing knowledge and building understanding, based on what children think about a topic.

Making what are known as "KW charts" is another way to get ideas out in the open. K stands for "know" or what children think they know about a topic. W stands for "what" or what we want to know more about, questions about a topic. Try to elicit ideas or questions from the entire class (teachers too) so everyone feels included. By creating a chart with the class, the teacher gathers the children's ideas to study and mull over as she works to figure out specifically what areas engage the children and what Big Ideas they might explore.

Consideration of Materials, the Prepared Environment, and Local Resources

As the Big Idea unfolds, it is a good time to think about what materials you already have in your program that could be used or repurposed for the Big Idea. Here is a list of materials/opportunities to consider:

- **Books** - What books does your program already have that fit the Big Idea? If your program is limited, work with your local children's librarian to find more titles. The books you want may need to be ordered from multiple libraries and could take time to arrive. What books do you have access to that you can explore in the meantime?

Figure 5 - Concept Mapping

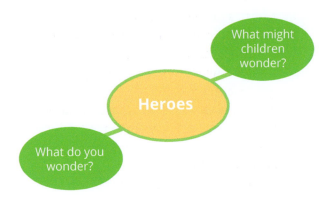

Children brainstorm about heroes as part of a study about how people help each other and the world.

Be sure to read the books to yourself and with your team ahead of time to support your own learning about a topic. Make decisions about how you will balance nonfiction and fiction titles, when you will read certain books, and how you will integrate books into your classroom book corner.

- **Manipulatives and Tray Work** - What materials does your program own that can be reconfigured for exploration? Do you have other resources locally such as other teachers, parents, friends, programs, museums, etc. that you could pull from? Start sending emails and making phone calls to find what you need. This is where Compelling Materials and Explicit Presentation support your work. Think about what will enhance your Big Idea and provide interesting opportunities for children to engage with materials that support discovery and learning about a topic. Think about when to offer these materials and what will be shown during large or small group times, or individually to children. Do you need to set up a specific shelf for tray work related to this topic? Or a center or area that becomes a hub for these materials? Plan, design and gather materials, and present them to children throughout your study.

- **Dramatic Play Materials** - Think about the materials that will enhance children's pretend play opportunities, indoors and out of doors. What type of dress up clothing or materials do you need in dramatic play for children to experience this topic? Do you need specific props to make it work? For example, if children are going to experience camping, do you have a tent you can set up for them to try? What other objects would be worthwhile for them to use? A flashlight, a sleeping bag, a hiking pack? Consider the Explicit Presentations you will give to support dramatic play scenarios and care of this area of your Prepared Environment.

- **Loose Parts and Recyclable Donations** - An investigation often includes some kind of representational aspect. Children in Reggio Emilia famously created an Amusement Park for Birds. Children focusing on the Big Idea "People wear different kinds of clothing," investigated the local laundromat and built a washing machine out of large boxes, found materials, and loose parts. "Loose parts" is a term that refers to a variety of materials offered and used freely. This could include found objects, recycled items, things from nature, and even manufacturing cast-offs. Loose parts can be used in as many ways as children imagine as they explore, move, manipulate, and build. Other terms such as "scrounge art" and even "maker spaces" can refer to areas of a classroom,

COMPLEMENTARY CURRICULUM APPROACH

or even a separate studio space, where children choose from a range of objects, tools, etc. to use in their own creations. Determine what materials you need and have access to (paper towel rolls, ribbon, newspaper, milk or orange juice container caps, etc.) to make the emergent topics and Big Ideas come alive in your art and building areas.

- **Local Resources** – Is there someone you could invite to your program who is an expert on the big idea you are investigating? Who could you write to? Where could you go to extend children's thinking and knowledge? For example, you may have a friend who is an avid bird watcher. Invite him to visit the classroom wearing his neutral bird-watching vest. He might show the children various field guides, bird whistles, and how to use binoculars. Perhaps like the teacher whose children were more interested in how their building was constructed than in community helpers, you'll invite a local architect to share knowledge about architectural plans. In this example, blueprints and other artifacts related to the visit were donated to enhance children's activity in the art and block areas. It is a good idea to issue these invitations early so you have plenty of time for long-term planning. Your interactions with experts should come towards the beginning of a study as a provocation and knowledge builder, not at the end. Remember, it never hurts to ask! You never know who might be willing to visit or host a field trip.

Invite people from the community to share their expertise with children early in a study, to spark questions and learning.

Sometimes, an idea you pursue with children just doesn't catch on or fizzles out over time. Even as you offer another direction, you find the children really are not invested in the topic. When a Big Idea does not ignite learning and children have lost interest, or you didn't quite catch what was important to the children, it is time to let it go and move on. Sit with your team and reflect on closure of the topic and where you will go next.

Make Connections Across Curriculum Areas

Many teachers have a favorite area of the classroom, and it is often the first place they go to add activities that relate to the Big Idea. For some it is dramatic play; for others it is a new art project, manipulative material, or book selection. Ideally, Big Ideas are the umbrella for a range of content areas. This means that the Big Idea should make an appearance in many areas of the classroom and children should have opportunities to explore the Big Idea through math, literacy, science, social studies, and social-emotional learning. Note that not everything in your classroom changes to align with the investigation topic. Other learning is happening too, and children need the stability of familiar materials and a range of materials.

Putting it All Together: The Pipes Story
This is an example of Following Children's Interests that takes the four intentions into consideration and is rooted in a Big Idea that truly captivated an entire classroom community—both children and teachers. The Big Idea presented itself to children through a shared experience during toileting. The teachers engaged in close listening, even during a plumbing crisis! As you read the "Pipes" story, you will see the process of Complementary Curriculum in motion.

The children were all in choice time when it happened. "Oh no!" a voice hollered from the bathroom. "The paper is coming back up!" A group of children ran to the doorway of the bathroom where their friend was now standing on the bench to avoid the flooding toilet. With a plunger in hand the teacher saved the day and the water receded. Later, when the children were gathered for circle, a flurry of questions emerged. "Why did the toilet do that? Why did the plunger fix it? Where does the toilet paper go?" The topic became so intense the teachers decided to grab notebooks and start to document the questions their students were presenting. As the students' questions unfolded, the teachers suggested they head to the bathroom to look inside the cabinets at the pipes; from there, they went to the basement. By the next curriculum planning meeting, the teaching staff thought that "Pipes" would be the next Big Idea. During the meeting they reviewed documentation of observations in the classroom and discussed the children's questions. In the process of studying the notes to find emerging interests, the teachers realized that the children were focused on a much bigger theme than pipes. The children were really curious about how the water moved from one location to another. With that in mind, the teaching team started to plan activities and lessons around the Big Idea, "Water Moves."

The teachers pulled the children together in a meeting to capitalize on their questions and reactions to the experience. With a large piece of chart paper, the teachers used two prompt questions and documented the children's responses: Why do you think the toilet overflowed? And why do you think the plunger could fix it? The children had wonderfully creative theories about how toilet clogs form and where the water needs to go when it happens. They demonstrated complex thinking about how the plunger worked. For example, one child explained that the "plunger had to go up and down fast to unstuck the pipe." The documentation confirmed that the children were interested in Big Ideas of water movement (going up or down) and understanding how water can get from one place to another.

Multiple Entry Points for Learning: Preparing the Environment

As the teachers gathered information for curriculum planning, they compiled all of their notes and questions from the children. They carefully considered what the children wanted to learn more about and the children's theories and understandings. The teachers wanted to ensure that they were building from the children's interests so that the focus would be on the children becoming strong thinkers. The intention was for children to cultivate the mindset of investigation and innovators via the pipe study. In order to do this, the teachers planned for multiple entry points and curriculum opportunities that included plumbing systems, pipes, water flow, suction, plumbers...the list went on. The teachers were excited to identify pipe opportunities throughout the school, including the playground. They thought carefully about all the areas of their classroom and the content each area housed, using a planning template to help organize their thinking and keep track of ideas. In using the intention of Compelling Materials, the teachers selected and prepared a variety of activities for all areas of the classroom that would give children opportunities to play, discover, and learn about the topic of interest.

The teachers also gave Explicit Presentations about the function of different kinds of pipes, the tools plumbers use, and science experiments involving suction and water pressure. At one point they used celery stalks in cups of colorful water to demonstrate naturally occurring pipes in nature! As the teachers began introducing new provocations, projects, tray work, and materials, they noted how each child chose to engage and experience pipes. For example, some children gravitated to the opportunities in dramatic play—building bathtub drains and fixing leaks. Other children were more interested in planning for a plumber to visit, while others were drawn to the individual experience of tray work with an eye dropper.

The teachers used a variety of Responsive Scaffolding techniques to support children's learning in all areas of the classroom. One child wanted to work with a p-valve pipe system constructed by a classroom parent. At first the child was happy to flush water through the piping system, but eventually the child wanted to experience a clogged drain. The teacher worked with the child to find a safe material to use to clog the demonstration valve so the child could observe its impact. Afterward, the teacher offered the child an opportunity to give an Explicit Presentation. The child was then able to scaffold his peers to have a turn as well.

Insights

You may have noticed many options and entry points with this project. When you intentionally plan for different choices or opportunities, the children will "take up" the offerings that best meet their needs developmentally. Teachers observed children's play and developed multiple Big Ideas as they watched and listened to learn what the children were thinking about as they talked to each other in their play. Teachers shared these Big Ideas with children to embark upon the study and grounded children's questions and activities. Some were simple, such as exploring how water moves. Other Big Ideas were more complex—pipes carry water, the shape of a pipe helps carry the water, moving water creates pressure. Teachers shared these Big Ideas with children to embark and to ground children's questions and activities.

Teachers decided to recreate the pipes scenario in the dramatic play area by offering versions of tools that they had seen with the visiting plumber. By doing this, they hoped to give children opportunities to experience a bursting pipe emergency, hands on tool experiences, and access to costumes such as tool belts and helmets. As they listened to children's questions and theories about how water moves through pipes, they decided to offer PVC pipes for exploration in the play yard and small pipes and funnels at the sensory table. All of this planning required a focus on the Prepared Environment and the materials needed, across content areas.

The pipes study demonstrates the way the four intentions come into play around a Big Idea. One shared experience of the flooding toilet led to an amazing learning opportunity filled with compelling materials, explicit presentations, and responsive scaffolding. This example shows how teachers can build the intentions around one big idea and how that idea can extend and meet a wide range of learners' needs.

Balancing Required Curriculum and Teacher Expertise

Some educators struggle with the tension between Following Children's Interests and predetermined curriculum. How to balance Following Children's Interests with required topics, as well as your own ideas, can take some navigating. Some programs may follow a mandated curriculum required by the school district or state. Or, perhaps you follow a particular curriculum that has a range of topics to be studied over the course of the year, or even each month. Some topics are rooted in program traditions that reflect the local customs or events, such as the seasonal opening of local community gardens, visits by the firefighters, or the annual parade. Your classroom may have a required theme of life cycles, for example. How might you mine this generic topic for Big Ideas? A few possibilities: Plants and animals grow and change. Things are born, they live, and they die. What's it like to be a baby? A grown-up? An elder? A provocation could be a series of photos of seasonal changes in trees, or a seed popping open and the first shoots coming out, and then observing and listening for how children interact with this provocation to learn what's interesting to them. What about your own ideas? You know your children well and have insights into their needs and interests.

You may have a personal passion that would be meaningful for a certain group of children to explore—your own expertise about a topic that layers beautifully with a classroom need. For example, a teacher who works in a city setting might come with a wealth of knowledge about farming and the seed-to-table concept. This could be an opportunity to contextualize food for children who don't see its origins beyond the grocery store. A teacher with deep knowledge and understanding about art and artists can bring that to a range of topics, from architecture to animals—introducing an artist's work, techniques, and life to complement any topic. Perhaps the artist becomes the focus of a project, with a Big Idea of "What is an artist?" When you introduce your own passions into the classroom, you give students the opportunity to find an emergent theme and to learn about you.

In both scenarios—required curriculum and teacher passions—the emergent aspect is central to the process. When introducing the topic, always find out more by asking children what they know and want to know about a topic. Watch, listen, and ask questions so you can find just the right entry point and direction. For the study, "Food grows and is harvested," you will need to consider: Do children want to plant seeds? Is this about cooking and eating for them? Understanding the machinery involved? Or learning about farm animals? If you begin with conversations with children, the direction will unfold—just be flexible enough to follow it.

Be Ready to Extend Learning

Teachers often wonder how long an investigation should last, and the answer is—it depends. Be ready to extend the learning, follow where it goes, or bring something to a close if children are ready to move on. Long-term investigations have the most impact when they can be explored over days, weeks, and even months. When you map out a concept or area of study with your colleagues and then with children, you begin to consider all the different directions a topic can take, so you can be ready to plan.

It is tempting to plan all sorts of nifty activities, way in advance. However, it is important to stay connected to children's evolving understandings and questions about the Big Idea, so you will want to plan only so far ahead; make an offering, and listen and watch to learn how the children invest in the experience. You will need to ask yourself: What new ideas or questions are emerging? How can the curriculum reflect that? Often the longer the duration, the more impact a topic of investigation and inquiry has on the students and classroom community. Now, your curriculum has moved beyond a short theme to a deeper inquiry where children make complex connections to their world and expand their knowledge.

Conclusion: Following Children's Interests in an Intentional Way

Many have embraced Emergent Curriculum as a mainstay of early childhood practice. This is a wonderful development and yet, some teachers feel that it means they should not plan too intentionally for children's learning experiences. They value play but might default to putting the same materials on tables each day, because they are not sure how or what to take up in children's experiences. Others adhere to predetermined curriculum because the openness of emergent work feels uncomfortable.

When teachers respond to children's interests, they engage in teaching practices that let children know that they are important and recognized. Working with children in this way connects classroom experiences to the greater world, and the process becomes more motivating and meaningful. Understanding and implementing strategies for intentionally following children's interests actually makes teaching easier and more fun!

Finding the Settled Classroom

Protecting Choice and Using Time Well

At the heart of the Complementary Curriculum Approach and the Four Intentions are two commitments: a commitment to children's right to make choices as part of their learning experience, and a commitment to children's right to have ample time to take up those choices. Choice and time offer children the opportunity to concentrate, develop a sense of order, become independent, and contribute to classroom life. Sharing control of learning with children affirms that they are competent and trusted in the classroom environment. All of this comes together to create a settled classroom with a tangible sense of community.

How can teachers better foster children's choice and decision-making? How can teachers manage classroom time throughout the days and weeks to provide ample space for children's exploration?

The following stories illustrate how teachers have used the Complementary Curriculum Approach to foster children's choice and to open up classroom time. We hope that their journeys help you find your settled classroom.

Why Choice Matters

In an attempt to manage behavior and teach particular content, teachers may unintentionally close potential entry points for children's curiosity, keeping their experiences tightly controlled. Picture children being directed to a table with one simplistic choice, and being told to play there until a bell rings, with no other options available until it is time to move to the next table. If there is little for children to take up in their classrooms, or if the space is designed to minimize interactions with the room as a whole, then children have to rely solely on adults to manage their movements and choices and guide their interactions with the materials they are offered. This makes for harried teachers who are busy serving up materials or figuring out how to direct children when they finish an activity and don't know what to do next. All this takes time away from meaningful interaction with children. In these tightly managed classrooms, children are often waiting—sometimes patiently, sometimes not. Imagine if, when you finished a project, you had to wait until someone told you what you could do next and wait for another person to bring your materials to you, while also being told where to sit and stay. You would probably get frustrated! Your motivation might diminish, and you would be tempted to occupy yourself unproductively with what was in front of you, even though you were not very interested in it anymore.

When children have the opportunity to make decisions about what they want to play with and choose the materials that have meaning for them, they become motivated to play purposefully (Wurm, 2005). Imagine the difference between a child in the block area who has been told to go there and who does not want to build, and a child who is eager to construct something she has been thinking about or who is drawn to the shapes and designs of the blocks. The first child will likely enter the block area, maybe make a big pile or stack of blocks, and then leave the area without really engaging in productive building, while the second child dives in with enthusiasm. When children engage in activities that are meaningful to them, they are motivated to broaden and deepen their experience.

In a settled classroom, children play purposefully and take time to explore ideas and materials. The curriculum is based on children's interests and needs; and children understand how and where to get materials for themselves, how to take things out and put them away, and how to take care of one's own body. Think of the many aspects of a child's day: when to eat, when to play, what to play with, when to use the bathroom, even when to get a drink of water. In a settled classroom, children are able to make decisions about when these things happen.

The ability to navigate a classroom is something children learn from teachers who support children's right to choice, meaning, purpose, and motivation. Dewey noted that adults have an obligation to guide children, but that does not mean that adults must *control* children. Montessori spoke at length about freedom within structures. This means that children will have some control over themselves and the choices they make. Part of the teacher's job is to model how to use materials and help children become good decision makers.

Martha: Tub to Tray Makes More Time for Play

Martha works in a large urban Head Start program. She has been a teacher there for 18 years. Martha's family has a legacy of teachers—her mother and grandmother were teachers. Martha works long hours, often arriving at the center at 7:00am and leaving at 6:00pm. Many of the children in her classroom stay five full days. She was completely frustrated. She was tired, burned out, and ready to quit.

Martha explained, "This just isn't what I thought it would be like. I have been teaching for years—I kept hoping it would get easier with more experience. I felt that I was losing my light and my passion for wanting to do this anymore." For Martha, the day in and day out of putting the bins of materials on the table was repetitive and boring for her and the children. Even the curriculum and books started to feel monotonous. Martha said, "I needed something new, something to jolt me out of this." She decided to try the Complementary Curriculum Approach.

Martha's classroom was divided into centers—Blocks, Art, Reading, Dramatic Play, and Table Spaces. Children had the option of going to these different areas but it never seemed to sustain them for very long. After learning about Compelling Materials

Martha started to look at her materials and how she offered them in a new light. She explained, "Now I look at the supply closet. I am getting rid of some things and thinking about materials in new ways. Before I remember looking in the closet and thinking, 'It's so boring.' For me this approach has given a lot of things in the closet a whole new life." Martha started to repurpose her classroom materials motivated with different ideas and seeing new opportunities. She describes, "See those little plastic links? Remember them? I used to hate putting them out because they would cause so much trouble. They would just tie each other up. We had to ban them! Now we look at them in a totally different way. With the trays it's giving the materials an entirely new life. I am creating work with less and getting more out of it!"

Over time Martha moved away from choices on the tables and added a variety of opportunities on shelves for her students. Some of the activities are in baskets and others are offered on trays. She explains, "I feel like there are so many more choices in my classroom now. The children are so busy and happy. I watch them and know more about what they enjoy and what they avoid. I am having so much fun redesigning activities that are connected to my Big Idea goals. I cannot even imagine going back to my old ways."

Martha's story illustrates the power of the Prepared Environment and Compelling Materials. Martha did something really important. She recognized there was something unsatisfying for her and the children, and she took the time to reflect on it and seek out new ways of working. Then she took small steps to prepare the classroom differently, curate materials, and design offerings in new ways. Now Martha is committed to supporting children to learn this way, interacting with materials of their own choosing and engaging with materials authentically. She sees how the children's enhanced engagement leads to deeper learning.

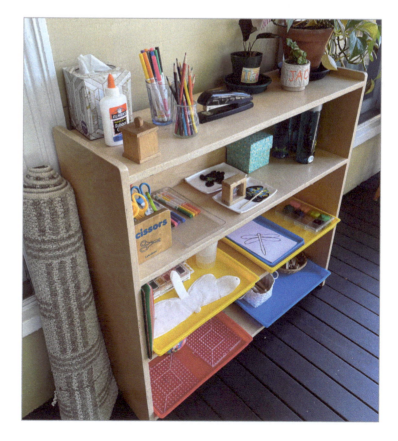

Eric: Making Room for Explicit Presentation Builds Access for Children

Eric works in a small nature-based private preschool in a suburb. With a class of 15 children and two teachers they have a manageable teacher-child ratio. The children go to school for 3-5 days a week from 8:00am-1:00pm. The program has been using a Reggio-inspired curriculum. Eric felt that while children in his classroom had plenty of opportunity for discovery and play, there was little room for teacher modeling or guidance. He felt confused about his role in the classroom and when to give children information about how to use tools and when to give lessons.

At first Eric was opposed to giving Explicit Presentations in his classroom. He was concerned that it would take away from the children's opportunities for discovery and choice. His classroom had beautifully prepared and open-ended spaces ready for children, but he noticed that children would often get silly, dump out baskets of materials, and not get the full benefit of the opportunities provided. In some cases, children were even mishandling or breaking materials. After learning about the Complementary Curriculum Approach, Eric decided with his co-teacher that Explicit Presentation was worth a try. They decided to present their class with a baby doll. They modeled how to hold the baby and treated the doll as if it were real, cradling its head and wrapping it gently in a blanket.

Eric explained, "What a captive audience we had. It was a different style for them, and they were so attuned." Eric noted that when they saw the children's reaction of deep interest and joy it was totally worth it. The children asked questions like, "Was it a real baby? How do you give the baby a bottle? Do you need to change the diaper?" The entire class was captivated and engaged. Eric prepared the Explicit Presentation to be more like a mini-drama/story. He described what he did in the classroom. "I told the children, 'I hear a baby crying...why is the baby crying? Are you hurt, are you hungry? Do you have a dirty diaper?'" He noted that he added feeling to

his voice and made sure that the lesson had a clear beginning, middle, and end. He was intentional with his language. "There was a lot of showing and listening. They were really paying close attention."

It was new for Eric's teaching team to use Explicit Presentation. He said, "Typically our group meetings were always on the fly. Now we have this tool that is so helpful. Now I ask myself, is this something the children need to know in advance? Do they need a presentation to learn how to do more?" Now Eric and his team are using Explicit Presentation more frequently to teach handwashing, tool use, and getting clothing on to go outside. He is also experiencing the impact Explicit Presentation can have on open-ended opportunities. "Sometimes it helps me slow down and reflect on what children need to learn. For example, we are wrapping a log with rope. Now I ask myself, "How am I going to teach making a knot?" I know that during the lessons I will need to be present and go slow. It's much more engaging with children when I am breaking down the activity.

When Eric embraced Explicit Presentation, he discovered that the children, once given foundational guidance, can make wise and informed choices about what they want to do. He worried that he would be squelching children's freedom by being too directive. However, because he knows and understands children, his interactions with them after an Explicit Presentation were rooted in Responsive Scaffolding that supported their exploration, interests, and success. When given guidance and responsive interactions, children are actually able to successfully navigate the freedom to choose.

Supporting Choice and Decision Making: Why Time Matters

Scheduling for Independence

Supporting children to make choices requires teachers to think intentionally about their daily schedules and to consider how they support children's right to choose and linger with materials. In order for children to have enough time to explore the choices offered to them, they need sufficient blocks of open time. An appropriate amount of time for classroom choices should be at least one to two hours, because that gives children and teachers enough time to dig into their endeavors. Montessori classrooms often have a two-and-a-half to three-hour work cycle or open play period. Long stretches of open play and exploration are also common in Reggio-inspired classrooms. The goal is that during choice time, children will take up and pursue a range of activities—independently, with peers, and with teachers—as opposed to being assigned to an activity by an adult.

Teachers often wish that children had more time for play, discovery, and choice. Initially, early in the year or when a new group comes together, play and discovery periods may be shorter. Children need some time to explore the classroom space and get familiar with how to move around, choose activities, and put materials away. Also, it could be that children have not yet developed the stamina to stay with an activity for a long period of time and might need more support to think about what they would like to do. The goal is to stretch the choice time, discovery time, center time, etc. so that children have enough time to access and settle into a range of choices.

It's important to develop a schedule that is both predictable and flexible. Children feel more settled in an environment where they know what to expect and know their needs will be met. When you are planning your schedule, is there enough time for children to really invest in an activity? How many transitions are there in a day? Which blocks of time on your schedule support child-led experiences? Do all children have to go to the bathroom, eat snack, or have lessons on materials in a whole group? Does your schedule currently require complex transitions rife with behavior management issues? How much time do children spend waiting for adults to do "for" them instead of children making their own decisions? As you reflect on the elements of your day, consider what you could change in your practice to give children the time they need to fully engage as

© Henry Frost Children's Program

learners. Teachers can choose to create more time for children to play, more time to connect in small groups and learn through deep inquiry and projects, and more opportunities to give some control of the day back to the children.

To support children's capacity to make and follow their own choices about what to play, teachers should help them find strategies for moving from one activity to another. This replaces the practice of ringing a bell every 10-15 minutes and instructing the children to move from one center to another. Part of the practice of Explicit Presentation involves teaching children how to transition from something when they are finished so they are able to determine for themselves what to take up next, and how long to use it. This means the presentation includes a demonstration of the exact clean up procedure, showing how to replace used items, reset the materials, wipe up any spills, close lids, etc. so something is ready for the next person who uses it. Once the materials are put away, you can take some time to ask, "Hmm, I wonder what you might like to do now?" or "Can I help you to make a new choice?"

In the same way that children feel a sense of empowerment by being able to take care of classroom materials, they also derive a sense of agency when they have the opportunity to make choices, have enough time to engage with materials, and are in charge of their own learning. Teachers benefit too from the additional time to observe children and support their work. All this contributes to what the settled classroom looks like—a place where children pursue their own interests, stay engaged with an idea or project, and persevere when their work gets challenging.

Here are a couple of stories that illustrate what is possible when teachers adjust the amount of time they allow for open play and the way they offer activities.

Elaine: Finding Time for Journals

Elaine works in a public preschool program in a densely populated city. The children in her class come from a range of racial, ethnic, and socioeconomic backgrounds. Most children attend school from 8:15-5:30, taking advantage of the district's afterschool program. Elaine had been teaching for five years and largely followed the practices of the veteran teachers in her building who moved children from center to center in 15-minute increments, ringing a bell when it was time to switch activities—which were almost always tubs of manipulatives on tables. But Elaine felt uncomfortable with how much "policing" she had to do during center time. Children weren't treating materials well and they struggled to engage meaningfully with the materials she offered at the four tables.

Elaine felt stuck. She really wanted to do journaling with children, creating a time when the children would draw and then dictate a story to her. This meant that Elaine would need to be with the journaling children, and the rest of the children would need to be somewhat self-sufficient and engaged so she could take dictation and talk with children about their stories. Elaine didn't see how she would have enough time in her morning for journaling, and the thought of children working independently seemed like an aspiration that was out of reach. Shifting her center-time routine felt overwhelming and counter to what other teachers in her building were doing. She had a few things to consider: how to get more time, how to support children's capacity for independent work, and how to launch a new literacy practice.

Elaine began each day with a half-hour morning meeting during which she took attendance and directed the children to add the date to a calendar, put weather icons on a weather chart, count the number of days they had been in school. Then they sang a song together, reviewed the letter of the week, and listened to a quick story. The children were very wiggly by the end of the meeting and Elaine spent time managing children's bodies and voices. "I feel like I just move through the meeting routines on automatic, trying to get through them so I can check them off the list." After teasing apart the aspects of the meeting, Elaine explored whether all those things really needed to happen during one long meeting at the beginning of the day. She decided that she and the children could read a story together more meaningfully at the end of the morning, after choice time and right before lunch. Counting the days of school took a very long time and wasn't really much fun for anyone—it could go. The weather routine was important only to the child who went to look out the window and then put a sticker on the weather chart; it would be more meaningful to talk about the weather before children went outdoors.

Elaine made these changes, and the new meeting lasted only fifteen minutes. Some time was found.

With this renewed approach to morning meeting, children had more energy when they got to center time. Now she had to rethink *that* part of the day to address the challenges that the activities provoked related to children's behaviors and an unsatisfying teacher role. Usually, Elaine would put one activity on each of the four classroom tables and rotate children through each activity center every ten or fifteen minutes. This meant that Elaine spent the bulk of her teaching time watching the clock and moving children between the stations. Her ultimate goal was to do some small group work with children, but her schedule and routines did not allow it. Elaine created a choice basket with a variety of items to get children started on their first choice for free play. After they finished with the first activity they chose, children could move freely to another activity where there was room to play. The new routines were explicitly presented, as were new materials. Elaine dedicated one shelf as a fine motor center with materials on trays that could be taken to an adjacent table. She also set up other centers in the room, including a "creation station" loose parts area with art materials that could be taken to a communal art studio table. After a few weeks, once the new choice routines were established and children were free to follow their interests, Elaine noticed that children actually stayed engaged longer at the centers they'd chosen than they had during her original fifteen-minute blocks of time. They were more focused in their play and had fewer conflicts. Her role could shift from

time-keeper or activity manager to someone who scaffolded their play responsively.

Now she had more time for small groups, and lo and behold, her choice time was now closer to 90 minutes, rather than 35-45 minutes. Elaine was ready to begin her journaling routine, dedicating 30 minutes three or four times a week, to work with children on their journals, giving them her full attention. While she did journals, the assistant teacher moved through the room, checking in with children to scaffold and support their play and help them change activities when they were ready to make a new choice.

Elaine's transformation of time allowed her to realize her longing to take up journaling with children. It also was a gift to the children: as they got better and better at successfully creating their own projects and pursuits, they experienced the satisfaction of perseverance and concentration and the joy of following their interests. Later in the year, Elaine was hunkered down at a table while children drew and dictated stories. "Look!" she said, "Aren't these stories amazing! I never thought I would have time for this or that the rest of the centers would work, but it is happening!" It was hard for Elaine to let go of old routines at first, but noticing and reflecting on children's successes encouraged her to commit to the adjustments.

Elaine's commitment to shifting the way she used time resulted in richer learning experiences for children. She wisely took the small steps necessary to make things successful for herself and her children. Elaine could not have made an abrupt shift to a 90-120 minute work/play period. Children and teachers need time to adjust and build stamina; being flexible supports the process of changing routines.

Jonathan: Smoothing Out the Edges of Clean Up Time

Jonathan teaches in a full day Head Start classroom in a public school. Many of his children are in the foster care system or are being cared for by grandparents. He is fortunate to have a team of family advocates to support him and the children. Jonathan has been teaching for 7 years and is a master planner and Compelling Materials designer. However, he finds that no matter how well choice time goes, transitions are challenging for the children. Jonathan feels that he gives children ample warning for clean-up time, but they still don't seem to know what to do and lose control, getting loud and wild.

Jonathan aspired to create clean-up routines that were a smooth, calm bridge from one activity to the next, but he was struggling. He tried different strategies like flickering the lights, timers with bells, and chimes to alert children, all of these accompanied

by a familiar cry from an adult that often rings out in classrooms: "FIVE MORE MINUTES!" Instead of being a signal for impending clean up and a transition, the alerts caused children to grow louder, to dump materials or to wreck what they were working on. The children quickly switched activities and started something else they couldn't possibly finish, and some children hid under tables. To move forward, Jonathan considered the following questions: "What do the children know about cleaning up? What does the clean-up signal really mean to them?" Children have to understand what they are supposed to do when it is time to clean up. First, Jonathan needed to decide what he wanted it to mean. Does clean up mean put things back in a tub? Return materials to shelves? Who puts what away? Does everyone have some kind of classroom job?

After Jonathan decided what he hoped the children would do at clean-up time, he thought about how he could communicate that it was clean-up time. Jonathan recognized that some children likely experienced the clean-up signal as an interruption and wondered if they would be able to come back to their work. He explored what signal he might use to let the children know it was time to clean up, and how he would teach the children about the signal. Since loud, frequent bells, buzzers, and voices raise children's stress levels, Jonathan explored options such as a soft bell, rainstick, or chime that would be less jarring than a loud, booming announcement. He determined that a child could be the bell ringer, and he would try a soft chime and whispering voice for signaling and supporting clean-up.

Jonathan began with an Explicit Presentation about what the chime sounded like, when it would be used, and what exactly children would do when they heard it. "I will use this chime when teachers and children have an important message to deliver. When you hear it you will freeze your body and your sounds so you can hear the message. It might sound like, 'Please put away all your work so it is ready for tomorrow, and we will meet on the rug.'" At group

Each child has a "save my work" card that they can put next to their activity to indicate that it is in progress and they will return to it.

meeting, children got a chance to practice by walking around the room, freezing when the chime rang, and listening for a message from whomever rang the chime.

After the Explicit Presentations, Jonathan and the children started working with this new clean-up practice. What a change it made! Everyone knew what to expect, and children were on a rotating schedule to be the "chime ringer." Children also began to ask to use the chime to deliver their own messages about sharing what they had done, such as a block structure or painting, inviting others to see and admire their work. The noise and stress level in his room went down during transitions, and children more easily moved into the next activity in a settled way.

Giving children an adequate amount of notice about an upcoming transition and delivering the message about the transition are important aspects of how you design the time in your environment. While it is important to alert children to a transition, the ways that teachers give the signal are often startling rather than supportive. Jarring loud signals and lack of explicit presentations about what to do and what to "clean up" sends children inadvertent messages beyond the message that clean-up time is coming. Here are some variations of what these clean-up announcements communicate to children and how children may internalize them:

> "Time to panic as I surprise you with this loud message while you are concentrating."
>
> "You don't have much time left so just crash your tower and walk away."
>
> "Hurry, hurry, hurry! Not much time left. Move fast, grab all the materials you need."
>
> "Just clean up now, because you won't have time to finish anyway. Throw everything in the tub as quickly and loudly as you can."

Think about clear language you can use to alert children to a transition so you can move beyond "Clean-up in five minutes" and communicate more accurately what is happening next: "Please finish your work, put it back on the shelf or in its tray, and head to the rug for meeting." While a five-minute warning can be helpful, also consider only ONE signal, with plenty of time for finishing work, putting away materials, and getting to next place or activity. Consider being proactive for children in block areas, art studios, and dramatic play so they get a personal message from teachers, earlier than the general announcement, to begin to finish their work, as these areas take longer to pack up. You might try giving out "save cards" with children's names and photos that children can put on an activity to save it so they can work on it again later in the day or the next day. The opportunity to save work and continue it later is important because it places children's need for continuity and order at the center of the learning experience. Children need time to wrap up activities, decide what they might want to carry over to the next day, carefully put away materials or reset an activity for the next play period, and move their bodies to wherever they need to be next. Managing transitions intentionally is a way that adults can communicate respect for children's work and share control of learning with children.

Conclusion:
Time, Freedom and Joy

Giving children choice and time in our classrooms is a crucial part of the Complementary Curriculum Approach and helps to create a settled classroom with a tangible sense of community. As a teacher, you work to improve the lives of children and their families. You want your school and classroom to be joyful places of learning that are engaging and fulfilling to you and your students. When children have opportunities to choose and the time to enjoy those choices, children and teachers have a sense of collaboration and mutual respect that creates a strong foundational learning experience for all.

A Closing Message

The voices of teachers we work with continue to resonate with us. We hope you are encouraged to consider how the Complementary Curriculum Approach could support you in your teaching practice. What are your next steps towards a settled classroom? They need not be monumental. If you read something in this book that calls to you, but it feels too large to implement, pare it back, do less—but do something! Small steps can lead to big changes for yourself and for your children. Maybe you start with some simple change to the environment. Maybe you design three Compelling Materials to add to your literacy or math shelves. Maybe you pick one material or routine to give an Explicit Presentation about. Whatever your entry point, remember that the Prepared Environment and the Four Intentions were meant to build on each other and overlap. Dig in, give yourself permission to be your best self as an educator, and reach out. Find time to reflect with colleagues. Find time for quiet reflection and setting intentions. Celebrate your successes by sharing photos, videos, documentation, and new ways of working with colleagues, families, and children.

At the outset of this book, we talked about the tension that exists between play-based, open-ended experiences for children and the increasing pressure to build skills. The Complementary Curriculum Approach demonstrates that you do not need to be caught in this divide any longer; it allows you to maximize children's learning potential and gives you the power to meet their needs. Create the beautiful spaces, offer the energizing choices, and seize the opportunities for playful learning that brought you into this field. We are excited for you to start on your journey with the Complementary Curriculum Approach. We hope that it reinvigorates your practice and, most importantly, supports your joy in the classroom.

References

Introduction: The Search for the Settled Classroom

Copple, C. & Bredekamp, S. *Developmentally Appropriate Practice in Early Childhood Programs (Revised Edition)*. Washington, DC: National Association for the Education of Young Children, 2009.

Derman-Sparks, L. & Edwards, J.O. *Anti-Bias Education for Young Children and Ourselves.* Portland, ME: Stenhouse Publishers, 2010.

Kuh, L., LeeKeenan, D., Given, H., & Beneke, M.R. "Moving Beyond Anti-Bias Activities: Supporting the Development of Anti-Bias Practices." *Young Children* 71 (1). (2016).

Early Childhood Legacies: The Influences that Shape Complementary Curriculum

Bodrova, Elena, and Leong, Deborah. *Tools of the Mind: The Vygotskian Approach to Early Childhood Education*. Upper Saddle River, N.J.: Pearson/Merrill Prentice Hall, 2007.

Dewey, J. *Experience and Education*. New York: Macmillan Company, 1938.

Edwards, C., Gandini, L., & Forman, G. *The Hundred Languages of Children: The Reggio Emilia Approach Advanced Reflections (2nd ed.)*. Westport, CT: Ablex, 1998.

Jones, E., & Nimmo, J. *Emergent Curriculum*. Washington, D.C.: National Association for the Education of Young Children, 1994.

Helm, J. H., & Katz, L. G. *Young Investigators: The Project Approach in the Early Years (3rd ed.)*. New York: Teachers College Press, 2016.

Katz, L.G., Chard S.C., & Kogen, Y. *Engaging Children's Minds: The Project Approach (3rd ed.)*. Santa Barbara, CA: Praeger, 2014.

Lillard, P. P. *The Montessori Classroom: A Teachers Account of How Children Really Learn*. New York, Schocken Books, 1997.

Lillard, A. S. *Montessori: The Science Behind the Genius*. New York: Oxford University Press, 2005.

Montessori, M. *The Absorbent Mind*. New York: Henry Holt, 1967.

Vygotsky, L. S. *Mind in Society: The Development of Higher Psychological Processes*. Cambridge, MA: Harvard University Press, 1978.

The Prepared Environment

Curtis, D. & Carter, M. *Learning Together with Young Children: A Curriculum Framework for Reflective Teachers*. St. Paul, MN: Redleaf, 2008.

Dewey, J. *Experience and Education*. New York: Macmillan Company, 1938.

Edwards, C., Gandini, L., & Forman, G. *The Hundred Languages of Children: The Reggio Emilia Approach Advanced Reflections (2nd ed.)*. Westport, CT: Ablex, 1998.

Flannery, M. "The Aesthetic Behavior of Children." *Art Education* 59(3), 33-35. (1977).

Kuh, L. (Ed.) *Thinking Critically About Environments for Young Children: Bridging Theory and Practice*. New York: Teachers College Press, 2014.

Lillard, A. S. *Montessori: The Science Behind the Genius*. New York: Oxford University Press, 2005.

Montessori, M. *The Secret of Childhood*. New York: Ballantine, 1966.

Tarr, P. "Consider the Walls." *Young Children* 59(3) 88-92. (2004).

Vecchi, V. "The Role of the Atelierista." Published by the Commune de Reggio Emilia, 1990. Retrieved from www.dcrealliance.org

The First Intention:
Compelling Materials: Designing for Choice and Discovery

Curtis, D. & Carter, M. *Learning Together with Young Children: A Curriculum Framework for Reflective Teachers*. St. Paul, MN: Redleaf, 2008.

The Second Intention:
Explicit Presentation: Teaching for Confidence and Competence

E.M. Standing. *The Montessori Revolution in Education*, New York: Schocken Books, 1969.

The Third Intention:
Responsive Scaffolding

Bodrova, E. and Leong, D. *Tools of the Mind: The Vygotskian Approach to Early Childhood Education*. Upper Saddle River, NJ: Pearson/Merrill Prentice Hall, 2007.

Vygotsky, L. S. "Play and its Role in the Mental Development of the Child." *Soviet Psychology, 5*(3), 6–18. (1967).

REFERENCES

The Fourth Intention: Following Children's Interests

Lesaux, N.K., Jones, S., Bock, K., & Harris, J. "The Regulated Learning Environment: Supporting Adults to Support Children." Young Children, 70(5), 20-27. (2015).

Cassidy, D.J., Mims, S., Rucker, L., & Boone, S. "Emergent Curriculum and Kindergarten Readiness." *Childhood Education*, 79(4), 194-199. (2003).

Chard, S., Kogan, Y., & Castillo, C. *Picturing the Project Approach: Creative Explorations in Early Learning.* Lewisville, NC: Gryphon House, 2017.

Finding the Settled Classroom: Protecting Choice and Using Time Well

Wurm, Julianne P. *Working in the Reggio Way: A Beginner's Guide for American Teachers*, St. Paul, MN: Redleaf Press, 2005.